SUCCESSFUL SALES MEETINGS

How to plan, conduct, and make sales meetings pay off

By Jim Rapp

Published by
The Dartnell Corporation
4660 N Ravenswood Ave, Chicago, IL 60640-4595
Chicago / Boston / London

Copyright 1990 The Dartnell Corporation
Printed in the U.S.A. by Dartnell Press
ISBN 85013-171-5

DARTNELL is a publisher serving the world of business with books, manuals, newsletters and bulletins, training materials for business executives, managers, supervisors, salespeople, financial officials, personnel executives and office employees. In addition, Dartnell produces management and sales training films and cassettes, publishes many useful business forms, conducts scores of management seminars for business men and women and has many of its materials and films available in languages other than English. Dartnell, established in 1917, serves the world's whole business community. For details, catalogs, and product information, write: THE DARTNELL CORPORATION, 4660 Ravenswood Avenue, Chicago, Illinois 60640—4595, USA—or phone (312) 561-4000.

This publication may not be reproduced, stored in a retrieval system, or transmitted in whole or in part, in any form or by any means, electronic, mechanical, photocopying, recording, or otherwise, without the prior written permission of THE DARTNELL CORPORATION, 4660 Ravenswood Avenue, Chicago, IL 60640-4595.

This publication is designed to provide accurate and authoritative information in regard to the subject matter covered. It is sold with the understanding that the publisher is not engaged in rendering legal, accounting, or other professional service. If legal advice or other expert assistance is required, the services of a competent professional person should be sought.

From a Declaration of Principles jointly adopted by a Committee of the American Bar Association and a Committee of Publishers

©Dartnell Corporation

About the Author

Jim Rapp is President of Outlook Associates, Alexandria, Virginia, a consulting, training, and publishing organization. Outlook's clients are primarily trade and professional associations, including:

> The National Association of Tobacco Distributors
> Delta Nu Alpha Transportation Fraternity
> National Retail Hardware Association
> National Office Products Association

Mr. Rapp is also a partner with Harper Administrative Services, Inc., Orlando, Florida, an association management firm. The Harper organization has as its primary clients the National Society of Sales Training Executives (NSSTE) and Transportation Clubs International.

Jim Rapp is an experienced trainer, specializing in sales and sales management. He is also a professional writer, with experience in course development.

As Director of Education for the 9,000-member National Office Products Association, he built the income of the department from $50,000 to nearly a million dollars in nine years. He pioneered the use of video instruction, developing a three-day basic selling skills course using this medium.

In addition to the office products field, Mr. Rapp has had considerable experience in the food industry, both as a retailer and as a salesman, sales manager, and sales training manager with General Foods Corporation.

He has written numerous books and self-instruction material for Addison-Wesley, Prentice-Hall, NSSTE and Bill Publications. He is now writing a booklet on key account management for NSSTE.

A long-time member of NSSTE, Mr. Rapp is also active in the American Society For Training and Development.

He lives in Alexandria, Virginia and maintains offices in Alexandria and in Orlando, Florida.

Contents

Section 1	Introduction	7
Section 2	Developing a Meeting Budget	11
Section 3	Planning the Meeting	19
Section 4	The Theme Meeting	31
Section 5	Getting Participation	39
Section 6	Announcing the Meeting	49
Section 7	Building Training into the Meeting	55
Section 8	Special Types of Sales Meetings	71
Section 9	Workshops and Seminars	79
Section 10	Humor in Sales Meetings	95
Section 11	Showmanship in Meetings	109
Section 12	Using Meeting Planners	119
Section 13	Speakers and Workshop Leaders	125
Section 14	Finding the Best Meeting Site	137
Section 15	Negotiating with Hotels	149
Section 16	Opening the Meeting	159
Section 17	Making a Presentation	165
Section 18	Arranging for Transportation	187
Section 19	Getting Meeting Rooms Ready	195
Section 20	Handling Food/Banquet Functions	205
Section 21	Managing the Entertainment	215
Section 22	Planning for Emergencies	219
Section 23	Handling Problem Individuals	227
Section 24	Closing the Meeting	233
Section 25	Evaluating the Meeting	237
	Index	245

©Dartnell Corporation

Section 1

Introduction

Why have a meeting?

That's a good question, and one that's coming under increasing scrutiny at top management levels these days. And it's a question not likely to go away soon, as management—large or small—faces increasing pressure to cut costs and become, as the takeover artists are fond of saying, lean and mean.

Okay, why indeed have a meeting?

Simplistically, the answer lies just where it did during the free-booting days of the '50s, '60s, and '70s—communication: the eyeball-to-eyeball situation where people with the same common goals thrash out problems standing in the way of achieving those goals.

Sure, in this age of instant electronic communication it isn't necessary to sit down in the same room with your peers and superiors to communicate. Or is it? We think it is, and so do most—if not all—companies in this age of instant satellite communication. There just is no substitute for group interaction, face-to-face. The question then is not, Why have a meeting but, *how many* each year, *where*, *when*, and *for what specific purposes*. The sections that follow will explore answers to these and other questions pertaining to meetings and their viability in terms of doing business in the space age.

While communication stands at the top of the lists of why to conduct meetings, there are other equally cogent reasons to hold meetings: for training purposes, to motivate a sales force, to introduce new products "in the flesh," and to achieve interaction in problem solving from top to bottom within a sales organization.

Meetings serve a salutary purpose in the following ways.

©Dartnell Corporation

Training Any educator at whatever level will tell you there's no substitute for the one-on-one approach to learning, which is just another word for training. The cold, impersonal connection between a memo writer or an instructor on a satellite hook-up and a salesperson is a fragile connection, as compared to a face-to-face connection in a meeting room.

Motivation No matter how brilliant your sales training materials are, or how often they are updated and distributed, they lack the power of the spoken word and the eye contact that goes with face-to-face contact. Motivation, according to the dictionary, means to impel and incite. And the best way by far to impel and incite is in person.

New product introductions It would seem obvious that the best way to fire up a sales force with a new product is to show them the product in person, not on a TV screen or in a handsomely illustrated catalog. Alas, far too many firms ask salespeople, for whatever reasons, to accept the wonders of a new product on faith alone. This is hardly a way to impel and incite enthusiasm, the critical ingredient in sales success.

Group interaction and problem solving In most tough sales situations, someone has figured out a way around the problem—or how to avoid it in the first place. That someone, like it or not, is one of your own salespeople, sitting right there in the second row at the meeting. His or her interaction with the group could produce an answer of benefit to everyone present. Also, of course, the experience of seasoned salespeople can be of invaluable assistance to younger employees or to those still in training. The best place for this interaction is the meeting.

The times are changing There was a time not too long ago when sales meetings, except in rare circumstances, were pretty much considered a paid vacation, a break from routine, and a time for endless conviviality. No more—not that today's version of the sales meeting is relentlessly stuffy, dull, and something to be endured. It is just that today's meetings have responded to profound attitudinal changes in society. Salespeople today, many of them young and upwardly mobile, need education in order to achieve that upward mobility. They know this

©Dartnell Corporation

and don't require force feeding when it comes to the raw material of education—information.

Thus, much of the old-time hoopla has gone out of today's sales meeting. There may be those who decry this trend, but there are a lot more who applaud it. A sales meeting is no longer a sort of roistering bonus from the boss, but rather a chance to learn and earn. And that's the point for many of the younger people entering sales forces. This, in turn, poses serious challenges to those who are in charge of meetings.

Meeting the needs of the new generation of salespeople will be a recurrent theme throughout the sections that follow.

All things considered

A meeting without an objective(s) is a meeting to cancel. It is a wise boss who asks right off, "What do we hope to accomplish by the meeting?" Your answer had better be to the point and specific; in other words, have *action objectives* in mind. For instance, your firm is a major factor in the decorative fabrics market and, mid-season, one of your mills has come up with a new weaving technique that allows for a more attractive product at a lower cost. The sales force must know, and fast. It is time for a meeting and an *action objective*: 400 new accounts before the competition catches on, which it is bound to do.

What are the benefits to be gained from the meeting in this example rather than, say, from a long sales bulletin with swatches of the new fabric attached? Well, how about those familiar words used above, *impel* and *incite*, and the action objective of getting more accounts in a hurry.

Your agenda for any meeting should *always* be as simple as possible, which is just another way of saying that it must be focused. You can't cover the waterfront in a single sales meeting; even if you could, you probably would lose the attention of about half the sales force at the end. Work from an agenda (no surprises, please), keeping in mind that the agenda must be focused and have an action objective as its centerpiece.

When you have your agenda, it's time to move on to the next consideration—accommodations for the meeting. These will depend, of course, on the size of the meeting planned, the hurry-up nature of the gathering, and the proximity of the sales force. Don't procrastinate on nailing down accommodations, once all signals are "go" for the meeting! Securing and reserving accommodations can be, and usually is, a time-consuming and frequently frustrating part of the entire sales meeting plan.

This brings us to another question in this introduction: Why use a manual in preparation for a sales meeting? After all, isn't it a relatively simple matter to get the salespeople together in some hotel meeting room, feed them, bunk them down, then do your best to impel and incite them? Those who have tried this off-the-cuff approach to sales meetings know the answer to this one: The answer is no, it is not possible. *Organization* is the key word here, and that's the point of this manual. Organizing—and using checklists to keep track of the myriad details involved in any sales meeting—is your only guarantee of achieving goals and of justifying costs involved.

Even with the best planning, no one can guarantee your meeting will draw plaudits from salespeople and boss alike, but without organization and detail planning, it's a safe bet your meeting will be a shambles.

The aim of what follows is to assist you in avoiding such disaster. Consider this a road map into the always uncharted territory of planning a meeting of diverse people with common goals.

©Dartnell Corporation

Section 2

Developing a Meeting Budget

Unless you are fortunate enough to work for an extremely enlightened individual, probably the first thing the boss will want to know about a forthcoming meeting is, "What's it going to cost?" Steel yourself for this one. It's a question you'll have to face even before queries as to what you hope to accomplish at the meeting.

There is little wonder that there is concern about meeting costs these days! Travel, site rental, equipment rental, food, and hotel costs have, along with everything else, skyrocketed in recent years. Moreover, these are only the up-front expenses involved in a meeting, be it large or small. The hidden costs are just as important, even if they may not require the immediate use of a checkbook. Hidden costs include such things as the downtime for the sales force, for you and other company executives in planning and implementing the meeting, and for a certain corporate inertia that prevails when most of the producers in any firm are attending or preoccupied with a meeting. Current competitive factors require constant minding of the store, for time is indeed money.

Basic budgeting considerations

There are two basic budgeting considerations involved in the planning of a sales gathering. First, there are the up-front costs, which include all the obvious expenses such as travel, hotel rooms, food, entertainment, speakers, etc. These are relatively easy to calculate, if difficult to justify. Second, there are the hidden costs, such as the downtime of the sales force while at and enroute to and from the meeting. These costs are not nearly as easy to calculate as the up-front variety. They can be subjective, with many variables. In

©Dartnell Corporation

preparing these costs, our advice is to err on the side of being generous; don't underestimate in this department.

However you go about budgeting for your meeting, just make sure that you don't leave out potential surprises, such as insurance charges at the meeting site.

Obviously, your budgeting in final form cannot take place until you have concluded other segments of meeting planning, particularly negotiations with hotel and meeting site personnel. You may have a ball park figure on such costs—and it's good to have one as a guide—but you can't nail down certain key costs until you have signed hotel contracts, airline and rental car commitments, etc. This is all the more reason why planning for a meeting or convention must be a long-range process. You can't be expected to work within tight budget restrictions for spur-of-the-moment gatherings. The hospitality industry just doesn't work that way these days.

Preparing the budget

After you have pulled together the logistics of the meeting, with commitments from all suppliers, you should prepare a detailed budget for management, including up-front and hidden costs. It may interest you to know that many experienced meeting planners build in a 10 percent contingency factor in order to come in at or under budget.

This budget should be submitted in as simple a form as possible. The budget proposal is not the occasion for razzle-dazzle or confusion. Keep it simple and understandable, relying as much as possible on simple forms. (Suggested forms for budgeting a meeting are included in Figures 1 and 2 on pages 13 and 14.)

Be sure your budgeting proposals are submitted to management far in advance of the meeting. Don't expect instant action on your proposals; you're not talking about peanuts and, except in rare circumstances, corporate decisions of this magnitude aren't made overnight.

Your meeting budget undoubtedly will generate a lot of discussion, both with your boss and with his or her boss. Rest assured that somewhere along the line the eagle eye of a comptroller

©Dartnell Corporation

Figure 1. Sales Meeting Budget (Up-Front Costs)

Meeting _____
Location _____
Dates _____

1. Meeting Room

    Rental $_____

    A/V (tapes, films, rentals) $_____

    Other sales aids (catalogs, etc.) $_____

    Stage costs (lights, sound, unions) $_____

    Shipping, assembly $_____

    Insurance $_____

2. Transportation

    Airfares (estimated) $_____

    Ground (taxis, buses, rental cars) $_____

3. Facilities

    Number of persons _____

    Rooms _____ x _____ days x $_____ $_____

    Meals _____ Breakfasts @ $_____

    _____ Lunches @ $_____

    _____ Dinners @ $_____

    _____ Banquet @ $_____ $_____

4. Support Services

    Speakers $_____

    Trainers (seminars/workshops) $_____

    Entertainment (cocktail parties, artists, flowers, room rental) $_____

    Gratuities $_____

    Total estimated cost (inflation factor noted) $_____

©Dartnell Corporation

**Figure 2.
Sales Meeting
Budget
(Hidden
Costs)**

```
1. Staff Time
    Executives _____ x _____ per hour x
    _____ hours                                              $_____
    Supervisors, managers _____ x _____ per
    hour x _____ hours                                       $_____
    Support personnel _____ x _____ per
    hour x _____ hours                                       $_____

2. Sales Personnel Time
    Number of salespeople _____ x _____
    hours x _____ *average per hour                          $_____
                                    Total hidden costs            $_____
    *Based on average per hour earnings of everyone on sales force @ 40 hours per week
```

type will more than scan your proposal. This is all the more reason to make your budget proposal as straightforward as possible and without surprises.

Remember that this scrutiny boils down to one basic issue: Will what's accomplished at the meeting justify the cost? This is a legitimate inquiry on the part of management and must be considered in all planning phases of the meeting, particularly in stating clearly the meeting objectives. Don't overstate. Set realistic objectives and phrase them clearly in an attachment to the budget figures.

Keeping a rein on costs

Anyone with experience in following meeting budgets through to their successful conclusion—that is, the planning and executing of a successful meeting—knows how frustrating the approval process can be. Attempt to avoid some of the more obvious financial objections by considering carefully *where to spend*.

We can't stress this strongly enough! Many otherwise solid budgets for meetings have become instantly suspect because of some quirky enthusiasm of the budget-writer. Your salespeople can get along without a banquet appearance by some expensive TV luminary.

Dramatic meeting highlights may play well at the banquet itself, but will draw chilly reviews at the board meeting of your firm.

Is it necessary to hold the meeting in season at a famous resort, when you could wait a couple of months and get the same service and accommodations at half price? No matter how lavish your meeting may be, it is always best to put your money where it is likely to count: meeting the objectives for the session. No one will cry poor-mouth when it comes to housing and entertaining the meeting participants, but there is a big financial difference between luxury and perfectly adequate accommodations.

The same thinking applies to good services at a meeting or convention. There is a big difference in the cost of specialty foods (and drinks) and menu items commonly available and served as part of the hotel's traditional menu. This is not to suggest that you take everyone out to McDonald's at lunch break, but merely that you don't allow the atmosphere and food to obscure the point of the gathering, which is the accomplishment of pre-set objectives, clearly articulated to management in your budget proposals.

If you are lucky enough to be able to splurge for your meeting, put your spare change on educational materials, effective speakers and workshop leaders, and pertinent audio-visual materials. In doing so, you'll avoid questions from the boardroom.

Furthermore, if you get the reputation within the firm of being conservative on meeting budgets, chances are that your proposals for objective-related expenditures will sail through with little or no question.

Getting the most for your money

Here are some areas in most meeting budgets that usually can be trimmed, or which at least offer possibilities for second thoughts.

1. *Travel.* This is an area of sales meeting expense that can get out of hand rapidly. Airlines themselves are often confused these days about fares and even their own so-called SuperSaver programs. If possible, work with a reliable travel agency as far in advance of the meeting as possible. Schedule

your meeting, if possible, during off-peak seasons and off-peak days of the week. Your savings in this area can be substantial. Also, book in group lots as much as possible and avoid individual fares when you can. Also avoid the everyone-is-on-his-or-her-own concept in getting people to and from the meeting. The same applies to ground transportation. Keep in mind that there's economy in numbers. *Get a reliable travel agent involved*, and do so early.

2. *Hotels.* Shopping around in the hospitality industry always pays off in planning a meeting. What are the local competitive factors? What are off-season, off-day periods? Work with local convention bureaus as a starter, then move to specific locations for comparative pricing. Shop around. Some fine hotels have been built in recent years in pretty strange locations. Favorable tax laws have spurred such development and, to get established, these hotels frequently offer outstanding bargains to meeting planners.

3. *Meals.* It pays to study this segment of your meeting plan with care. If your sales force is national, chances are that some of the trendy (and expensive) ideas that have crept into hotel cuisine in recent years will not appeal to your staff. You can be basic in this category without being dull and please the majority of the people attending. Most hotel food service departments price per person, and there is a wide variation in per person cost depending on menu offerings.

Where not to skimp

Here are some areas in meeting planning where it does not pay to skimp.

1. *Speakers.* Nowhere is it more true than in this category that you get what you pay for. Again, shop around! Many top-notch universities and colleges maintain speakers bureaus. Educators with knowledge of your field and/or problems probably are available nearby and more than eager to speak at your gathering. These college bureaus can provide resumés for

your perusal, along with fee schedules, usually much lower than the famous names on the lecture circuit.

2. *Workshop and seminar leaders.* These people don't come cheap. This is no place to skimp either, for bombastic or ill-informed trainers can undercut an entire meeting.

3. *Audio-visual aids.* While there admittedly is a lot of technical razzmatazz in this field today, don't pinch pennies. Concentrate on what is *pertinent* to your meeting, not on what is trendy or merely amusing. If you feel, for example, that a film is needed to assist in a new product presentation, have the film done by professionals. The same goes for training aids. There are many good sales training films available, but the best cost money. Don't settle for second best when it comes to films or tapes. This of course means that you have to turn into something of a film critic long before the meeting, or rely on the word of an associate or friend.

The overriding consideration in budgeting for a sales meeting is to make your budget realistic, and not only because it stands a better chance of approval. You yourself must be satisfied that the cost is balanced by the accomplishment of objectives. A good rule of thumb in budgeting is: If I were the boss, would I take a chance on this? If the answer is yes, go ahead with your planning; if the answer is no, get out the red pencil and go over your budget again.

If the meeting you are planning is months off, keep in mind the need for an inflation factor in your figures. Inflation now is running at about 6 percent a year. Factor this (or the applicable figure) into your budget.

Figures 1 and 2 on pages 13 and 14 show a couple of easy budgeting forms to use in preparing your meeting. You can also use them as checklists during planning.

Section 3

Planning the Meeting

If you find yourself in a position of planning a meeting as just one part of your job (and this is the case in a vast majority of firms), there may be times when you wonder how you ever got involved in such a time-consuming, detail-laden operation in the first place. Thus there is a temptation—a real one—to wing it for the next sales meeting. Odds are overwhelming that you'll find your wings clipped when you adopt such a casual approach to what is probably costing the company a bundle of money and time.

The best meetings—those that accomplish something on schedule—are those that appear to be effortless as they play out, with no gaffes either in meeting flow or arrangements. This doesn't happen by chance.

Good meetings require professional planning. The aim is to make everything appear to be effortless. You and your assistant(s) may be the only ones who know what effort and planning it took; but then, a great actor doesn't remind the audience after each performance how much time he or she has spent planning every move on stage. It's called professionalism.

In planning the meeting, here are the key guideposts.

Set your objectives First, what do you hope to accomplish with the meeting? In other words, what are your goals?

Education Probably the most common goal at meetings boils down to education. Any firm these days, large or small, feeds and grows on constant change and improvement in product or manufacturing technique.

©Dartnell Corporation

No business today stands still. It's a constant push for new and better products. In most businesses, the advent of a new line is a natural (and necessary) launching pad for a meeting. The aim, of course, is to educate the sales force in the new product and achieve sales dominance within the product category.

Lead time in the introduction of new products varies from industry to industry, but the principle remains the same: The sales force must be educated in the new line and in its ancillary promotional and advertising back-up.

Two-way communication Another common and important meeting goal is two-way communication: The salespeople learn what's going on at headquarters (recent decisions, policies, and procedures) and management learns what progress is being made toward objectives, what's needed to move things faster, and receives recommendations on mid-course adjustments.

While the above are the most common meeting goals, other goal considerations are the following:

Planning and coordination This involves such topics as work load matters, possible changes in departmental responsibilities, and reassertion, if necessary, of who is in charge of what and why.

Reassurance This is another word for gaining support for something already on the boards by trying to resolve issues or concerns and by explaining and informing.

Let's get them on our side This involves explaining things that are on the horizon and soliciting ideas and recommendations *before* the fact.

What's the problem? This need not—and should not—be an exercise in negativism. Instead, it means to lay a problem(s) right on the table and solicit views on correctional means. This is usually a good way to clear the air, as well as to allow management to snuff the spark before the bonfire.

Any or all of the above can be goals for a meeting, but, depending on the size of the new line or the extent of communication

©Dartnell Corporation

difficulties within the firm, don't just tack on meeting goals in your preliminary outline to please the boss.

After you have jotted down your meeting goals, ask yourself the hard question, "What are the action goals of the meeting?" You don't want your meeting to end up as just a lot of talk, or looking at pretty slide shows of the new product!

Let's say the primary goal of the meeting is education—the introduction of a new product that requires the prominent display of promotional material in each territory. Is it enough just to say that the display is key to the successful kick-off of the new product? Or to suggest jokingly that the promotional materials will do no good in the trunk of the salesperson's car?

The action objective for each rep is to name his or her key accounts, the ones where, at a minimum, the materials must be on display. After each rep names key accounts in his or her territory, keep the number noted/recorded on a slip of paper. When it's all over, total the number of key accounts and announce the minimum number of display stations for the new product. That's an action objective, not just feigned enthusiasm when you show the mock-up and suggest how much it will help. Get the salespeople to commit themselves verbally so they'll later take action.

After you set out the objectives of the meeting and establish specific action and goals, move on to the next key guidepost.

Planning the heart of the meeting

The first consideration here is meeting content or agenda. Without fail, the most effective meeting is the one that has an established agenda communicated in advance. The agenda should tie the meeting to company goals and provide precise direction during the meeting itself.

It's also a good idea to solicit ideas or suggestions for the agenda from as many people as possible within the organization. This may sound like a formidable, if not messy, undertaking. However, you'll probably be surprised at the responses. Most will zero in on common concerns within the organization. There will, of course, be the odd

Figure 1. Agenda Requests

```
Please submit agenda topic suggestions for our meeting _____
                                                        (Date)
at _____.
                        (Location)
1. _____.
2. _____.
3. _____.

_____    _____    _____
        (Signature)                  (Date)        (Dept.)
Use separate sheet to expand on above, if necessary.
Please return to_____, _____ by _____
                    (Your name)               (Dept.)      (Date)
```

agenda request, but the majority of your responses will be similar, even if phrased differently.

And in soliciting agenda ideas, don't intimidate your potential respondents by asking for written essays. Many articulate people are cowed when asked to put their thoughts in writing. Make your agenda request memo as impersonal as possible. The best way to accomplish this is to supply each potential respondent with a simple form, much like the one shown in Figure 1, above.

When you get these responses back—and this should be done well in advance of the actual meeting—it is a relatively simple matter to read through them carefully to determine the patterns of concern and/or interest among managers and other personnel. This is a far more efficient method of setting your agenda than having informal chats in hallways or encouraging long memos from respondents.

Further, this technique is invaluable in giving everyone a sense of participation in the meeting *before* it convenes. It brings the team approach into planning the meeting at its earliest stages, which in turn gives you a head start on making the meeting a success.

What emerges from your study of suggested topics for the agenda will be the preliminary or general format of the meeting. This can be a simple general list of what will be going on and in what order. For example, your preliminary list for a one-day meeting might read as follows:

©Dartnell Corporation

1. Welcome and orientation
2. Guest speaker
3. Break
4. Workshops
5. Lunch
6. Tour of plant
7. Coffee break
8. Panel discussion and workshops
9. Question and answer period
10. Summary
11. Announcements
12. Banquet

This preliminary agenda, of course, will vary from firm to firm, and will be revised and expanded as plans progress into the final agenda, which is much more detailed and will likely be subject to change right up until the meeting starts.

The final agenda should include specific times for each agenda item, and every attempt should be made to enforce these times. Normally the tendency is to crowd too much into an agenda.

Because of this, even slightly exceeding the time limits can find you far behind by late afternoon, and audience interest will lag. Make it clear to all concerned that it is essential to stay within time allotments. Your final sales meeting agenda, with specific times, should emerge in something like the form shown in Figure 2, page 24.

This same form can be used if you plan your meeting to run more than one day. It is a valuable guide to keep in front of you at all times during the final planning and during the meeting itself. Copies of this final agenda should also be in the hands of all your assistants and all guest speakers as a silent reminder that they, too, are working within strict time limits.

You might think—and this is a common error—that once the meeting adjourns, your work is over. It's not that easy. A big part of your work remains—evaluation of the meeting itself.

©Dartnell Corporation

Figure 2. Sales Meeting Agenda

Meeting date _____ Hours _____ Location _____

Meeting theme _____

Time	Topic	In Charge	Equipment
A.M.			
8:30- 8:45	Introductions	Me	
8:45-10:00	New product	Me	Slides, flip chart
10:00-10:30	Coffee break	Me	Coffee, rolls, milk
10:30-11:30	New product test market history	Product mgr.	Overhead projector
11:30-12:00	Questions on new product	Product mgr.	Flip charts
P.M.			
12:00-1:00	Lunch	Joe Jones	
1:00-1:30	Sample presentation	Me	
1:30-3:00	Role playing - new product	Small groups	Video recorder
3:00-3:15	Coffee break	Joe Jones	
3:15-3:45	Review quotas, explain contest	Me	
3:45-4:00	New policy on cars	Me	
4:00-4:30	Open discussion	Me	Flip chart
4:30	Adjourn		

Doubtless your gut reaction will be on target in determining whether the meeting met its goals or even approached them. But how do the other participants feel about the meeting? How can you learn to avoid the mistakes that occurred? The best way, and the simplest, is to solicit the views of the participants in the form of a post-meeting evaluation questionnaire. Again, you will be involving others in the entire meeting process and, more importantly, preparing an invaluable record for sharpening up future meetings.

A simple form, such as the one shown in Figure 3 on page 25, distributed at the final coffee break, likely will provide you with information you need, even if you would perhaps prefer not to know some of it.

©Dartnell Corporation

**Figure 3.
Meeting
Evaluation**

Help us improve future sales meetings. Please complete this form and leave it on the table at the end of the meeting. You needn't sign your name.

1. Overall reaction to this meeting _____

2. What are the two most important ideas you got from this meeting? _____

3. What topics would you have liked more time for? _____

4. What subjects could have been shortened or dropped? _____

5. What subjects would you like covered in future meetings? _____

6. What concepts, approaches, and techniques do you plan to use in your own territory? _____

7. Please rate these factors:

	Good	Fair	Poor	Comments
Meeting overall	☐	☐	☐	_____
Visuals, props, etc.	☐	☐	☐	_____
Take-home material	☐	☐	☐	_____
Meeting room	☐	☐	☐	_____
Meals, breaks	☐	☐	☐	_____
Hotel	☐	☐	☐	_____
Speakers	☐	☐	☐	_____

8. Additional comments _____

©Dartnell Corporation

In addition to setting up and following a pertinent agenda for your meeting, the next most important step in the planning process is selecting a location and appropriate accommodations for the meeting. As anyone who has planned meetings can tell you, this process is sometimes a minefield of broken promises, inefficient service, and one snarl after another.

It thus behooves anyone responsible for a meeting, large or small, to pay strict attention to the details of *when* and *where* and, not least, of *how much*.

In site selection, there is no substitute for a personal far-in-advance inspection of the premises. Such an inspection should encompass a number of subjective considerations you might not think have much to do with a sales meeting.

For instance, you can avoid a lot of grief by the briefest of visits to the average convention establishment. You can find out a lot by just peeking into a set-up meeting room. You can find out a lot, too, by having lunch in the establishment's dining room or coffee shop. Is the help efficient? Courteous? Well groomed? Is the food edible, average, or prepared with obvious professionalism? These are all judgments we make in non-professional capacities every day, and they are considerations that carry over into group dining. It's not hard to spot surly service, inefficiency, or unsanitary conditions. Nor is it hard for a stranger to sense the tone of any hotel or meeting center. Ask to see, as well, an average bedroom. The manager will be delighted to show you one, if there is nothing to conceal.

Other elements besides ambiance go into the site selection process, not the least of which is pricing on the volume of business you control. This consideration will be discussed in more detail in Section 14.

If you are unable to run a personal inspection of the proposed meeting location, it pays to ask around among colleagues or friends about a suggested location. Chances are, someone you know and respect has had an experience, bad or good, with the site under review.

©Dartnell Corporation

**Figure 4.
Checklist for
Meeting Site**

1. Easy to get to?_____
2. Within budget?_____
3. Clean, comfortable rooms?_____
4. Good meeting room?
   (Bright, well-ventilated, spacious)_____
5. Quality food?_____
6. Courteous, clean staff?_____
7. Comfortable chairs?_____
8. Equipment available?_____
9. Easy parking?_____
10. Good airline connections?_____
11. Recommended by recent user?_____

Use a simple checklist like the one shown in Figure 4, above, when sorting through site possibilities.

If your answers to these eleven checkpoints are yes, you have what you need in terms of location and should open negotiations with the management. Keep in mind that most major meeting centers (and even some in the offbeat category) are booked long in advance. Don't expect to get what you want if you put off making reservations until the last minute. Most major convention hotels require at least six months' lead time for an average-sized convention or sales meeting. Some require even more than that if they are in a particularly desirable location.

Keep in mind, too, that most major cities in the country are eager for your business, so eager in fact that many cities fund meeting and convention bureaus. Usually a full-time director and his or her staff are more than eager to put you on the right track in the selection process for a meeting site. These bureaus are listed in phone books of major cities, available in most libraries. A preliminary call to these bureaus can save a lot of time, plus give you a quick overview

©Dartnell Corporation

of space and price considerations without lengthy and time-consuming correspondence.

Another good thing about checking first with the local convention and meeting bureau is that you are dealing with a relatively objective person in terms of site desirability. Doubtless your contact will tout his or her city, but when your needs are known, you are likely to get the straight stuff on each hotel.

If we have made what might be construed as an excessive point about the need for formal planning of a sales meeting, we make no apologies. More sales meetings have gone awry from off-the-cuff planning than for any other reason.

However, planning the sales meeting need not be as onerous or intimidating as it first seems. The trick is to put simple forms and procedures in place early on, then keep on top of them as the day approaches. It is a serious mistake to think you can carry all the details in your head. No one has that good a memory, for one thing, and any sales meeting, to be successful, must be a team effort.

That is why the final checklist on the agenda, with precise timing spelled out, is essential. Use of the form suggested earlier in this section (Figure 2, page 24) will save you hours of agony on deadline day.

As a cross check for yourself as deadline day approaches, it also is a good idea to keep in front of you what we call the Have I Forgotten Anything Review List, shown in Figure 5 on page 29.

In effect, this is a laundry list of just about everything you will need for any sales meeting. Probably you will use only a small portion of it for your meeting. However, when you've got only hours before the big event, it can be both helpful and reassuring to run your finger quickly down the list to see if you've forgotten anything.

©Dartnell Corporation

Figure 5. Have I Forgotten Anything Review List

PARTICIPANTS
- ☐ Notified in writing: date, location, hours
- ☐ Told what to bring
- ☐ Have directions to site
- ☐ Meeting schedule conflicts?

MEETING SITE
- ☐ Sleeping rooms reserved
- ☐ Meeting room
- ☐ Meeting room seen, dimensions
- ☐ Meeting room set-up arranged
- ☐ Meeting supplies
- ☐ Meeting equipment
- ☐ Meal functions
- ☐ Coffee breaks arranged
- ☐ Meeting room location posted
- ☐ Material shipped or taken to site
- ☐ Estimated cost of meeting
- ☐ How to handle messages

PREPARING MYSELF
- ☐ Agenda complete
- ☐ Prepared opening remarks
- ☐ Written speech or made notes
- ☐ Practiced what I will say
- ☐ Anticipated questions
- ☐ Visuals prepared, films, slides
- ☐ Handout material prepared
- ☐ Samples, sales aids ready
- ☐ Meeting evaluation form
- ☐ Prepared case study
- ☐ Prepared for adequate participation

EQUIPMENT
- ☐ Video equipment
- ☐ Slide projector, slide tray, remote extension
- ☐ 16mm projector, take-up reel
- ☐ Overhead projector
- ☐ Tape recorder
- ☐ Screen
- ☐ Chalkboard
- ☐ Easel with paper pad
- ☐ Lectern
- ☐ Spare projector bulbs
- ☐ Sound amplification

SUPPLIES
- ☐ Markers, chalk, eraser
- ☐ Paper for notes
- ☐ Pens, pencils (sharpened)
- ☐ Badges
- ☐ Table name cards
- ☐ Masking, scotch tape
- ☐ Gaffer's tape
- ☐ Extension cords
- ☐ 3-prong adapter plugs
- ☐ Blank tape, cassettes
- ☐ Blank overhead transparencies
- ☐ 3-hole punch
- ☐ Stapler
- ☐ Pocket knife

©Dartnell Corporation

Section 4

The Theme Meeting

The so-called *theme* meeting has long been popular with sales managers and salespeople alike, and for good reason: Use of a theme provides instant focus to any sales gathering. Everyone knows right away where the concentration of the meeting will be.

The only problem with relying too much on the theme technique for a meeting is that it may, if abused, go against the grain of some of the younger people on your sales force.

There is a fine line between the intelligent use of a meeting theme and overuse. In other words, the medium can too easily become the message. Many of the tried-and-always-thought-true theme meeting techniques of the past are, put bluntly, out of date.

This is not to claim the theme meeting is in any way passé. However, the trick is to hold down the heavy doses of hokey stuff when theme meetings are called for. There's little more painful than to see the younger and more sophisticated people on your sales force squirming through time-worn sales exhortations built around a theme.

What this amounts to is a truth all sales managers are facing these days: The young people entering sales are, generally, better educated than those of a generation ago and far more sophisticated. This requires much more subtlety in conducting theme meetings than was necessary even a couple of years ago.

Advantages Before we consign theme meetings to the trash bin as outmoded (or too difficult to handle in a subtle manner), let's first consider their major advantages and perhaps attempt to restructure their virtues in terms of today's sales realities.

©Dartnell Corporation

First, what are the virtues of a theme meeting?

1. An appropriate, viable theme for your meeting can be like the core of the gathering. Everything else is built around this core concept. This makes planning the meeting far easier for you, since the theme unifies the entire proceeding, thereby reducing the chances of straying off the topic throughout the meeting. In sum, a themed meeting stands a good chance both of staying on course and on time—no small considerations in any meeting.

2. Done correctly (which is to say without cornball gimmickry), the themed meeting can provide solid advance interest by the sales force. A good theme can start your salespeople planning what to say *prior* to coming through the doors for the first session of the meeting.

3. A themed meeting can and should tackle a major problem or development within the firm head on and deal with it at length. The editing process that takes up so much time at an unthemed meeting is done in advance. The theme announces right off: "Here's what we are going to discuss and thrash out." Since by naming a theme you have automatically provided a meeting focus, you have allowed the salespeople to gather their thoughts in advance for the meeting. This without fail encourages good participation. A theme frequently offers many good ideas for improving performance in a given area all through the company.

Selecting a theme

Care needs to be taken in selecting a theme. If your choice is too restrictive, it may not even be germane to what's actually going on within the company. If it's too broad in concept, why bother with the theme at all? Most important of all, never inject a theme into a sales meeting merely to fit it around some clever presentation technique or some new item of electronic gadgetry that's just come on the market. The theme, to be effective, must come from the dynamics of your own firm. It might reflect a problem that needs addressing, a product that needs major introduction, or even a major policy that's being changed or abandoned.

The theme also should be of the variety that lends itself to expansion as the meeting assumes its own dynamics. One that is too restrictive will, again, have to fall back on gimmickry to stay alive for the course of a meeting.

Search for a thread of common and shared interest in the theme you select. It should be broad and pervasive enough to allow for give and take during the entire meeting.

One of the most workable themes in today's business climate is overcoming competitive factors from foreign markets. Virtually every industry in the land faces direct or indirect threats from foreign competition. It is a theme, too, that's discussed informally in living rooms every night on network news. Everyone has an opinion in general terms on how to overcome this competition, but few zero in on how his or her own company can cope.

Concepts for theme building

Most themes, including the one above, are universal and can be built around the following concepts.

1. *Know your industry.* This broad concept can be narrowed down to specific themes by concentrating on any or several of the following: distribution in the industry; this is your company; who are our customers?; who are our competitors?; company policies regarding the industry; who are our suppliers?; the salesperson's job in this industry; how to quote prices and discounts; the salesperson as credit adjustor; the salesperson as merchandiser; entertaining customers; how to develop enthusiasm. Examples include New Leaders in Transportation; Take the Hi-Tech Highway.

2. *Know your products and services.* This broad concept suggests the following specific themes: how to sell specific products; sources for product information; how to use sales aids; what to stress in a product; coordinating delivery; what services are we selling?; selling the firm's services as well as the

product. Examples include Service Comes First; On-Time Delivery Every Time.

3. *Know your customers.* This broad category is one of the favorites for themed discussions, with some of these specifics as possibilities: what makes someone buy?; what is the real buying motive and how to find it; problem solving as a sales tool; planning sales as opposed to impulse buying; why do people have favorite salespeople? (this one is always good for lively discussion); why should someone buy from us?; what should I know about the customer?; keeping customer records. Examples include Creating Customer Confidence; Satisfied Customers Buy More.

4. *Locating prospects.* Here's a category that often intrigues the livewires on your staff, those who are never satisfied with the same old rounds and routines. In other words, the people you always wish you had more of. Some specific theme possibilities are: where to look for prospects and leads; how to qualify prospects; what should you know about a potential prospect?; how to use letters to get prospects interested; prospecting by phone; cold canvass methods; how to get to see the right person; getting customers to help you locate prospects; getting and following up on leads. Examples include Warm Up Your Cold Calls; Scientific Selection Succeeds.

5. *Getting a sales interview.* Some specific theme possibilities in this category are: preparation for the interview; how to get past the receptionist; how to determine the prospect's needs; how to start an interview; how to duck problems with the purchasing agent; favorite ice-breakers with new prospects; how to deal with diversions; how to get a phone interview; the first three minutes; getting to the person who can say yes. Examples include First Impression Success; Planning Produces Profit Pay-Offs.

6. *Making the sales presentation.* This is another broad category

that can be broken down into a number of specifics, all of which are likely to elicit positive response. Some specific theme suggestions: how to plan your sales story; how to build the sales talk; favorite sales presentation; formulas for a good sales presentation; how to sell benefits, not things; how to see the prospect's point of view; how to make a survey; elements of a proposal; how to use samples and gifts; the art of showing; using the right words in selling; demonstrating the product; controlling the interview; selling creatively; warming up the prospect; how to avoid price-only selling; how to present quality; how to listen; how to ask pertinent questions. Examples include Quality Leaders; Seven Ways to Sell More.

7. *Handling objections.* Here's a broad category that offers a wide range of specific themes, among which are: how to get to the real reason for the objection; how to prevent objections; turning objections into sales; most common objections and how to handle them; how to prepare to meet objections; changing objections into questions; the art of listening; the customer sometimes isn't right; overcoming product objections; how to handle put-offs and stalls; how to lick friendship competition; overcoming ties with other salespeople. Examples include Going From No Way to I'll Pay; Higher Price Has Its Privileges.

8. *Closing the sale.* Mighty treatises have been written on this most important weapon in any salesperson's arsenal, so it is little wonder that themes related to the topic engender lively participation at any sales meeting. Here are some specific theme suggestions: trial closing; closing techniques and how to use them; favorite closing techniques; what to do when the prospect doesn't buy; writing the order; closing on resistance; recognizing signs and signals from the buyer; encouraging the buyer to buy now; helping the prospect to buy; how I lost that sale; how I won that sale. Examples

©Dartnell Corporation

include Getting to YES; Moving Mountains to Motivate.

9. *Building good will.* This general theme also produces some meaty meetings: the necessity for follow-up; what to do between sales calls; how to build a personal reputation; how to entertain customers; handling complaints when you are not around; building repeat sales; turning a sometimes buyer into a regular customer; keeping the customer sold. Examples include Our Customers Are Job 1; Pampering Pays Off; I ♥ My Customers.

10. *Time and territory management.* Most professional people, whether in sales or any other field, soon find out that time is not only the enemy but that it is a non-renewable resource. Some specific themes that will help everyone in the room are: time—your most important resource; how to make more calls; planning for long-term success; getting the most out of a territory; classifying customers for profitable calls; frequency of calls based on customer potential; daily and weekly sales planning; keeping records for proper territory management; analyzing sales records; regaining lost customers; use of the telephone as a sales aid; mining your territory; when to stop calling on a prospect; writing letters that sell. Examples include Tell and Sell By Telephone; New Routes to Success.

11. *Price, discount, and credit matters.* This nitty-gritty general category offers all sorts of opportunities for specific themes, but generally the trick is to steer the discussion off the negatives. Some suggested specific themes are quality versus price selling; credit and the salesperson; discussing price with the customer; government regulations on pricing; discount policies of your firm; how to handle discount competition. Examples include Discounts Mean Dividends; Collect Early, Sell More!

12. *Advertising and sales promotion.* Here's a broad category that invariably gets things moving fast, maybe because everyone

considers him or herself an ad manager, or at least superior to the one currently holding the title in the firm! You'll get a lot of "if only" talk on this one, but is that bad? Probably not. You'll also probably get a lot of good ideas from the line. Try to have your ad manager and some people from the agency present to listen in on these specific themes: how to use our sales promotion materials; is our ad campaign getting through?; how to use the ad theme in selling; is the customer aware of the advertising?; how to make effective use of co-op ad programs; how to police co-op ad expenditures. Examples include Sell the Sizzle; Tie-In to TV Testimonials.

Focusing the theme

Once you have chosen the theme (or themes) for the meeting, the problem is how to boil the concept down to easily understood terms on which you can hang the main ideas you wish to get across.

The first thing to do, then, is to take the theme and give it a zingy handle—a few words that get the idea across, even though the idea itself may be relatively complex. In sum, illustrate your theme.

If, for example, the theme centers on the need to fill expanded quotas in a line, you might choose Over the Top for your theme focus. This allows for various illustrated materials, slogans, and graphs to set the tone for discussion of the theme as people enter the meeting room for the first time. You can also build around the Over the Top theme with a variety of other visual techniques, such as the use of huge thermometers on the stage. Even training games that move the mercury to boiling can be devised, but the gimmicks in themselves must be buttressed by solid discussion of points raised as the game unfolds. Prizes work well in the Over the Top format, but care must be used to assure that not only the glib participate.

Very likely, the most important thing to remember in bringing off a themed meeting is to know when to lay off the gimmicks and dwell on the facts that tumble forth from the stimulation of the gimmicks.

Suggested themes

Here is a list of themes that you may wish to consider. Keep in mind that a theme can be very narrow, such as listening, closing, planning, etc. Other possible themes include:

©Dartnell Corporation

- Enthusiasm
- Warming up Cold Calls
- Teamwork
- A Salute to Our Customers
- Knowing Our Competitors
- Merchandising
- Look Good, Feel Good, Be Confident
- Selling Service
- Problem Solving
- Christmas in July (or some other month)
- Hawaiian Holiday
- Back to the Basics
- Being Creative
- Return to the '50s
- Breaking New Ground (Getting New Customers)
- Time (importance of, time to think, time control, time is money, etc.)
- Quality Counts
- Sale themes (old-fashioned sale, holiday sale, anniversary sale, etc.)
- Slogans as themes (Let's be No. 1, Sell the Sizzle, Go for the Gold, etc.)
- Movie titles (Gone with the Wind, The Orient Express, Casablanca, etc.)
- Break the Bank
- Game show titles (Jeopardy, Wheel of Fortune, Hollywood Squares, etc.)
- Let's Go Fishing (for new accounts)

The themed meeting, almost by definition, requires a skilled organizer and a person running things who doesn't get carried away by the props or the game itself.

Regardless of the theme, remember that a feeling of involvement and participation by every salesperson is the key to the successful use of a meeting theme.

Section 5

Getting Participation

We've come a long way from the days when sales meetings were run in an autocratic manner, with participation not only unwelcome from the floor, but actively discouraged.

It wasn't too long ago, in fact, that any sales manager who tolerated participation was suspect. How well we remember one sales manager of our acquaintance who used to open his sales gatherings by saying, "First off, let's understand at the start that I'm not running a democracy here." This sales manager was, we might add, highly regarded and highly successful, *back then*.

Today, and even he admits this, our sales manager's chances of running a successful sales meeting with such an opening remark would be nil. His salespeople might sit still after such an assault, but they wouldn't be with him. Those not resentful (probably the minority) would be suspicious.

The new trend is toward openness in meetings, where sales rep participation is not only solicited but sometimes required. The main reason for this is that generally we live in a much more open society than we did a decade or so ago. Young people are trained these days to question, to get in their two cents' worth. The flip side of this coin is, or should be, that once you get in your two cents' worth, you are responsible for carrying through on any program adopted from your wisdom.

Why participation? Why do you need participation? (Participation is defined here as orderly, not negative.) First, participation all along the line makes achievement of company objectives easier and thus the meeting more

©Dartnell Corporation

effective. Let's say the objective is a 12 percent increase in sales in the coming year in one specific product line. You, as sales manager, may feel that this can best be accomplished by the simple (on paper) expedient of setting a 12 percent quota increase on each salesperson.

But is it that easy? Of course not, even if sales managers in the old days tended to think it was. Rather than receiving a dictate from on high—and getting on with the meeting—this is the time for participation from the sales force. Several of the people may already have saturation or near-saturation distribution of the product in question. The problem, then, is not opening new accounts, but any or all of the following: poor advertising and promotion support, delivery problems, quality problems, bad packaging, unrealistic pricing, poor distribution. Allow anyone who wishes to expound on any or all of these possible deterrents to the objective to do so. There will be more than one, so be prepared. Make notes as the salespeople sound off, allowing for certain exaggerations and even finger-pointing. Through it all, stick to your guns about the necessity to meet the 12 percent goal.

When this winds down, it is possible (even probable) that you will have heard every reason in the book as to what needs to be done to meet the goal. But is that bad? Certainly not. In the first place, you will have determined areas where corrections are necessary. Most of all, you will have actively involved each person in the room in meeting that 12 percent sales increase. In other words, you have promoted enthusiasm and interest in the objective by hearing all ideas on the subject. These people now are *involved*, and not just passive participants in some mysterious company goal.

Granted, this technique of achieving participation gets you into a lot more work than the old no-democracy-here method, but it stands a far better chance of focusing on and achieving objectives.

The trick, as mentioned earlier, is to achieve participation without inciting anarchy. Aside from a few born dissidents in any organization, most salespeople are possessed of good manners and a sense of fairness to one another and to management. Those who haven't tried full-hearted and sincere participation may be in for a surprise at how reasonable (and understanding) sales reps can be.

©Dartnell Corporation

When you open the meeting to participation, you disarm the most vociferous dissidents.

Planning for participation

In achieving constructive participation, it is necessary to plan for it well in advance.

Determine the goal

First, it is necessary to have one primary goal in the meeting. You court chaos by pressing too many objectives at any one meeting. Select a primary goal for full-scale participation: how best to market a new product; how best to reinvigorate an old, reliable, and dull product; how best to overcome a competitive threat.

Once you have settled on your primary goal for participation, it is essential that you publicize the meeting as far in advance as possible, listing what will be under discussion and at which points participation will be requested. This will give all involved an opportunity to think over the problem before sounding off at the meeting. Your participants, in effect, will do their own editing, saving you a lot of time.

Involve your salespeople

To avoid the pitfall of sounding autocratic, it is a good idea to involve your salespeople in the planning of the meeting, particularly in what they would like to focus on at the meeting.

Do this before your agenda is cast in concrete. A simple form mailed to each salesperson well in advance of the meeting is an orderly way of keeping tabs of what's on the minds of your sales force. You might like to use a form such as the one in Figure 1, page 42, to help ensure participation.

It may not be possible to bring up many of the suggestions you'll receive, but chances are you'll discover a common thread of either concern or information in these responses, one that perhaps hadn't crossed your mind. Be sure to plan for open discussion of this issue at the meeting.

You should further involve the sales force as much as possible in site selection, distance to get to the meeting, and days of the week most convenient to be away from the territory. The more you can involve the salespeople in every phase of the meeting, the more

**Figure 1.
Topic
Suggestions
for Meeting**

```
I would like to have the following topics discussed at our forthcoming sales meeting,
in order of descending importance:

  1. _____
     _____

  2. _____
     _____

  3. _____
     _____

  Additional suggestions_____
  _____
  _____

  _____          _____
         (Signature)                     (Date)
```

successful the meeting likely will be. The trick is to maintain control and efficient planning while at the same time making each person who will be attending feel as if he or she is very much a cog in the wheel.

Another vital way of achieving a sense of togetherness—and getting some of the work off your own back—is to assign specific meeting projects to individual salespeople.

Each person within your organization is very likely an expert at something pertinent to the organizing or conducting of a meeting. You are probably aware of these individual skills. The more meeting-related projects you can assign to individual salespeople, the more participation you will have. There is no question that most people respond well to responsibility, particularly motivated salespeople.

How you handle making the meeting assignments depends on how well you know your people. If you know someone well, you can write a simple personal note saying, "I'd appreciate it if you'd give me a hand by making sure that the audio-visual equipment is in place and functional at the meeting." If you don't know the person too well, more formal instructions would be in order. Be sure you keep a checklist (see Section 3, Figure 2) as to who's in charge of what.

Even during the actual meeting, when unexpected situations arise, you can do a lot to ensure participation by calling on someone in the sales force to handle the situation. This is an effective way of not only talking about participation, but of getting it. Another truth, of course, is that most people want to be needed.

Ensuring participation: Techniques

One should be careful, however, to avoid playing favorites or sticking to the old reliables when seeking rep participation. *Everyone should be involved*, which is easier said than done in large meetings. However, there are a variety of proven techniques available to ensure almost 100 percent participation in even the largest meetings.

The workshop

The first such technique is the workshop, or problem-solving session. There's hardly a problem around that doesn't lend itself to solution via workshop discussion.

Done correctly, a workshop session has four basic steps:
1. Defining the problem
2. Getting all the facts together
3. Framing the solution or solutions
4. Testing the solution or solutions

Usually each group will come up with different but similar methods of solving the problem. The interaction that takes place in discussing the solutions will benefit all the groups.

The buzz session

Another good way of achieving participation, particularly in large groups, is the buzz session, which normally is conducted by breaking the group into smaller groups of four to six people. The group appoints a captain, who is responsible for conducting the session and for reporting the group's findings.

The various groups are given specific problems and allocated a period of time to reach a consensus on a solution or solutions. After each group has made its report, the person conducting the meeting holds a critique of the problem and its solution.

Buzz sessions and workshops differ in that buzz sessions usually come up with a wider variety of solutions than do workshops, which are more structured by definition. Thus, the critique session by the sales manager must be handled with considerable tact. There is a tendency at the conclusion of buzz sessions for each group to feel its solution is the most appropriate, or the only one. Actually, this is rarely the case. Any or all of the solutions might prove workable.

Role playing

Role playing is also an effective way of gaining meeting participation. This amounts to setting up a situation—based as closely as possible on actual events—and then assigning sales representatives to act out the solution.

Those who take part in this little drama need have no acting ability. They should simply be themselves in an imaginary situation.

As a method of exploring situations in which the reactions and feelings of individuals are involved, role playing is especially effective.

For example, role play is much better than lecture for bringing out the real reasons for resistance to change.

In role playing it is important to stop the drama as soon as the objective has been reached. People tend to become restless and inattentive once the crisis has passed. The critique in role playing sessions is particularly important because there is a tendency for each group to overlook the forest for the trees in evaluation of what went on—to focus on how well the objection was overcome rather than focusing on the method that was used to overcome the objection.

Asking questions

Good old-fashioned questions can also be a lively method of securing participation, but there are some tricks in this, too.

First, be sure you develop a technique to ask questions properly. Some tips on this are:

1. Write each question on the board.
2. Allow some "thinking time" before firing your first question.
3. Don't call on participants in rotation; select respondents at random throughout the room.
4. Don't play favorites by calling on only those you think might have the answer.
5. Go over the question if it is ambiguous or unclear. Give an example to clarify the meaning.

Follow-up is essential

A big part of the work in encouraging participation is the follow-up involved. It is almost better to return to the old authoritarian ways than to neglect the necessary follow-up. What is more disheartening to a salesperson than to feel that his or her ideas have been ignored? It's even more demoralizing to learn that nothing has happened after ideas were solicited. Thus, as one idea after another pours forth at the meeting—and they will—make sure you make notes and don't just casually agree, or worse, become defensive.

After the meeting, go over all the information you have gleaned from the participation session and assign objectives, suggestions, etc., to the proper people in the organization for either responses or action. The next very important step is to develop a sales bulletin in which all suggestions are identified and answered. For example, it may not be possible to change the packaging at this time (state why) or it may not be possible to switch the emphasis of an ad campaign already in place. Conversely, it might well be possible to correct or switch course as suggested at the meeting by the salespeople.

The point here is to let all who attended the meeting and participated know as soon as possible what came of the suggestions. This turns sales meeting participation into a continuing and productive exchange, and keeps all eyes on the 12 percent goal.

The form shown in Figure 2, page 46, is one you might wish to use to keep track of the remarks made at participation sessions and to show what was done about them.

Meeting evaluation

It is a good idea to have two evaluations, the first at the end of the meeting and the second after the salespeople have had time to implement the programs discussed at the meeting. In Section 3 you will find a simple evaluation form for the salespeople to use at the conclusion of the meeting. This also will contribute to a sense of continuing participation on the part of those present. But one caution: Don't use a form such as this if the group is small (say 10 or below). The idea that you might recognize an individual's handwriting will mitigate against frankness.

©Dartnell Corporation

Figure 2. Checklist on Meeting Objective

Idea	Action Taken	Persons Responsible	Follow Up (Days)

©Dartnell Corporation

Figure 3. Self-Evaluation Checklist

		Yes	No
1.	Was my primary goal accomplished?	☐	☐
2.	Did I get through the agenda?	☐	☐
3.	Did the meeting start and end on time?	☐	☐
4.	Was the audience interested and attentive?	☐	☐
5.	Did the audience leave in a good mood?	☐	☐
6.	Was everyone prepared, including myself?	☐	☐
7.	Did I select the right visuals?	☐	☐
8.	Were there any problems with the visuals?	☐	☐
9.	Did I keep within my budget?	☐	☐
10.	Was the meeting room satisfactory?	☐	☐
11.	Any problems with meals and coffee breaks?	☐	☐
12.	Am I satisfied with the participation of my salespeople?	☐	☐

As for your own evaluation—most important—you very likely have a valid gut reaction on how things went. Figure 3, above, shows a checklist you might find useful in determining just how it went.

Encouraging participation at sales meetings today is of paramount importance. If nothing else, it will improve general attitudes within the organization.

©Dartnell Corporation

Section 6

Announcing the Meeting

It should go without saying that any sales meeting is a semi-public event, not a secret among you, your secretary, and the boss. Therefore, you might be surprised at how many times sales meetings are called on extremely short notice, even when there's not a hint of a crisis on the horizon. There are times, of course, when there's a need for a hurry-up sales gathering. Examples include the introduction of a radically different product or a switch in company sales policy. These occasions are, however, rare.

Most firms, in fact, have long-standing sales meeting dates, depending on market traditions involving new additions to the line. These dates vary little from year to year, with the meeting usually taking place within a week or two of the previous year's meeting date.

However, even in these cases, what everyone wants to know, and on the button, is *when*. This is easy enough to understand; everyone these days has several lives to live, professional, personal, and leisure. It takes considerable juggling for even the most organized person to keep all these demands on time meshing properly.

In sum, the more advance notice you can give on the exact time and place of the sales meeting, the better. Those who call hurry-up sales meetings are likely to be considered suspect by the very people they are attempting to motivate. They also are likely to be roundly detested by the families of their salespeople.

Moreover, there frequently are very good reasons why a rep shouldn't drop everything and rush to a meeting. For example, his or her territory may be undergoing some important buyer changes, and

©Dartnell Corporation

the rep's on-scene monitoring of the situation may be critical in meeting sales objectives.

Announce your meeting early

While there may be no perfect time for everyone to come to a sales meeting, one thing is for sure: you'll get less flak about timing if you inform everyone as far in advance as possible. This includes exact dates of when the firm traditionally has sales gatherings. It is not enough to answer a question about the meeting date with, "Oh, some time in mid-June, just like always."

The sales bulletin

Most sales managers with good track records start planning the next sales meeting the day after everyone heads home, at least in terms of where it will be and on what dates. As soon as the dates are finalized (which will probably entail a considerable amount of jockeying at top levels), get out a sales bulletin right away with the news. This is a bulletin that should stand on its own, and it should be brief. Don't hide the date among routine announcements. If you don't cry wolf in every sales bulletin, turning even the most mundane pricing change into a blizzard of exclamation points and capital letters, you'll get the necessary attention by a few simple stand-alone sentences such as these:

Sales Bulletin 34

Mark your calendar now. Our next sales meeting will take place (date) at company headquarters in Minneapolis starting at 9:30 a.m. The meeting will run two full days.

This announcement, or one this simple, should go out *at least three months in advance of the meeting,* or earlier if you can nail down the dates.

To build up interest, it is a good idea to fill in details in sales bulletins as you assemble actual details of the meeting. Always repeat the exact time, date, and place of the meeting.

These advance teasers of the meeting should get more detailed as the process moves along and as your plans for the meeting become increasingly organized. However, if you have some surprise (pleasant or otherwise) for the meeting, save that for the meeting itself. Don't

©Dartnell Corporation

give away your second act climax before the meeting, and particularly not in a sales bulletin.

As the date of the meeting approaches, you will be in daily contact with many of the regional people, either on the phone or by memos. Talk up the sales meeting in these informal encounters and answer questions as they arise. Although the questions will be many and varied, answer them all. This is a good way to create a climate of interest and involvement in the forthcoming meeting.

There is a fine line, however, in all this. Be careful not to build up expectations to the point that the actual sales meeting itself becomes anti-climactic. Don't oversell, just inform.

A key part of preparing the troops for the big day is to encourage preliminary participation in the sales meeting planning. This is discussed in detail in Section 3, where you will find a handy form for use in soliciting agenda ideas. Return of this form by each rep acts as an indication that he or she knows the time and place of the meeting and will be on hand, with no excuses.

Publicize your meeting

There are also outside sources which come into play in informing everyone about your forthcoming sales meeting. Most of these come under the heading of publicity.

Publicity isn't nearly as mysterious as commonly assumed, nor as unpleasant. It is a tool valuable to both the originator and to the receiver—that is, to your company and to the media. In fact, the media would be lost without a certain amount of valid publicity flowing across desks daily. What the media are after is news, and your sales meeting date, place, attendance, and speakers very definitely qualify as solid news.

If you are fortunate enough to have a major ad agency, you will have access to a skilled publicist, one who knows his or her way around the media.

If you are winging it on your own, don't worry. Securing good and adequate publicity for your meeting is not as difficult as you may think.

In the print media, there are two targets for your meeting news:

the trade press and the consumer press. The trade press—the variety of specialized publications devoted to news of your particular industry—is eager for meeting announcements. Most have a special section devoted to just such happenings. And most industries of any size at all have several journals devoted to specific industry problems, personnel changes, etc.

The consumer press is the daily newspaper you read every day in your hometown. It is of general interest and does not zero in on any particular industry and its concerns.

The news demands of the trade and consumer press are the same in function, but different in approach. The trade press generally wants all the information it can get: details, details. The consumer press wants the bare bones or facts, but not too much detail.

Thus, in publicizing your meeting, it is necessary to prepare two separate press releases—one trade and one consumer.

The release for the trade press should be as detailed as possible, but devoid of vague wording. Your chances of getting your release into print as written are far better if you just stick to the facts and steer clear of all unnecessary adjectives.

Here's a possible format for a trade press release announcing your forthcoming sales meeting:

> Joe Jones, sales manager of the XYZ Company, Minneapolis, announced this week that the company's annual sales convention will be July 18-19 at the Hyatt Regency, Minneapolis. About 200 sales representatives of the firm are expected to attend.
>
> "Topping the agenda at the two-day conclave," Jones said, "will be discussion of increasing foreign competition in the multi-cell battery aspect of the firm's production."
>
> "Main speaker at the gathering," Jones said, "will be John W. Martin, Assistant U.S. Secretary of Commerce and a former resident of Minneapolis."

Further information, written in the same straightforward style, can be amended for the trade press release. Provide anything of interest to the trade, without giving away any secrets.

The same release, or a briefer version, can be used for the consumer press, but playing up the angle that the Assistant Secretary of Commerce will be the main speaker.

It is important to mail all the press releases on the same day. Include a contact name and phone number in case the editor desires further information or wishes to clarify a point.

The most important thing to remember in preparing your own press releases, trade or consumer, is to avoid flowery and unnecessary language. You'll be wasting your time in doing so and will build no press contacts that could be useful later on.

Publicity avenues to pursue also include radio and television stations. All of these outlets have news editors, and they, too, are eager for valid business news. The technique is the same, but remember that radio is audio and TV is visual. So, if you have a high-powered guest speaker, such as a prominent government official, alert the TV news editors far enough in advance so that they can make their camera set-ups and decisions about coverage early in the day. You stand a better chance of getting live coverage if you conduct these negotiations personally on the phone with individual news editors.

Whatever happens, don't get pushy in your quest for publicity. What you have will be used—if it's news. And sales meetings *are* big news for newspaper business pages, as well as for radio and TV business coverage segments.

The best way to handle publicity is to make sure you have something to say in the first place. Tossing your firm's local weight around doesn't wash in many newsrooms and, in fact, can backfire badly later on. Be cordial and, most of all, informative. Keep your releases simple and avoid unnecessary superlatives.

Section 7

Building Training into The Meeting

There's no argument anymore about the need for training sessions during any sales meeting. The only question is, How much training is needed and how should it be structured?

Obviously, the schoolroom approach to training generally won't work at a sales meeting. You'll have an audience, but the built-in resentments of "back in school again" are likely to overpower the training content.

The best technique, and there are a variety of ways to achieve it, is to make the training as painless as possible, meaning as non-academic as possible. Training ideally should be one of the fun segments of the meeting, meaning that you and your assistants will have to resist the temptation to get the training over with as fast as possible by the excessive use of chalkboards and pointers.

Why is training such an essential ingredient of any sales gathering? The most likely answer is that the need for training is the very reason the sales meeting was scheduled in the first place. Training is at the heart of effective selling; it stands at the top of the merchandising pyramid, outdistancing even such important considerations as building enthusiasm, buttressing teamwork, and stressing company loyalty. These latter considerations all follow in the wake of a trained salesperson.

Most sales meetings focus on line introductions, scientific breakthroughs, or some facet of a product line that is genuinely new and therefore an unknown to the sales personnel in terms of what it is and how to sell it.

©Dartnell Corporation

Management, to capitalize on the potential of a new product, the development of which likely cost a bundle, must further invest in seeing that the salespeople know what they're talking about when they go before the customers. Not only must reps be trained in the new product, they must also be trained in how to present the new product most effectively. This is the basic challenge of virtually all sales meetings.

The needs of the salespeople are centered on product education and on how best to present the product. The needs of management are centered on how to make the product a success. The lubricant in this mix-match of needs is training, best carried out at a sales meeting. All the sales bulletins in the world are no substitute for a hands-on training session at a sales meeting.

Considering the time limitations of most sales meetings, you'll find that much of your sales meeting will be structured, by necessity, around training, which needn't be as dull as it sounds.

First, most salespeople are in the top bracket of the general population when it comes to alertness. They are fully aware, even subconsciously, of the old saying, "The more things change, the more they change." To stand still on old products and concepts in today's marketplace is to lose ground. All your sales personnel know that; they are eager for a new, freshened product and are receptive to any ideas that will help them sell the product. Because of this, your job of structuring the sales meeting around education is a lot easier than it seems at first glance. But you still have to avoid the pedantic approach to sales meeting training; preaching and exhortation may have their place elsewhere, but not at a sales meeting. Then what form should training take at a sales meeting?

Training techniques

What follows is a discussion of major training techniques.

Lecture

The very word *lecture* has negative connotations, so by all means avoid its use in circulating your meeting agenda. Whatever you call it, a talk to any group of people to impart information is by definition a lecture. There's nothing wrong with a lecture, assuming it is prepared (and delivered) by someone who knows what he or she is talking about. Remember, a lecture is not a speech, even if the two can at times overlap in content and purpose. It can be said that a lecture is a speech by an expert and, as such, should be as devoid of gimmickry and obtrusive witticisms as possible.

Frequently a lecture is an effective way to impress on the salespeople the importance of a new product and the amount of time and effort that went into its development.

The lecture as a training device is most effectively used in conjunction with other training techniques. The lecture should 1) impress, 2) inform, and 3) illuminate. It should not bore. Here again the chance of boring salespeople with a preliminary lecture on the details of a product from whose sales they will be making their livings is remote. Moreover, if the lecturer is regarded as an in-house expert, you'll find the attention quotient for this segment high indeed.

It is best when using an opening lecture format to follow the lecture immediately with a question and answer period, while ideas are fresh in everyone's mind. It is a good idea, too, to record this question and answer give and take for circulation later to the sales force.

Most experts—if they truly are expert at something—tend, unfortunately, to think everyone knows almost as much as they do. It can be like coming in on the second act of a play: you know how it all turns out, but how did it start? That is why a lively question and answer session at the end of a lecture is all important. These sessions can be training at its best.

When selecting your lecturer, resist all blandishments from whatever source to use the boss as the lecturer. Although he or she might well be the world's ranking authority on the product in question, it is all but impossible for a boss to provide the objectivity required of a lecturer. It is far better to employ the services of the actual designer of the new product or of a well-respected merchandising expert, as your lecturer, unless, of course, the boss is an unusually self-effacing person who is more widely regarded for his or her creative skills than for administrative skills. This would be a rarity in today's highly structured business climate.

If there is time, combine the lecture in a two-part training session, the lecture and the workshop/seminar.

Workshop/ seminar

Following the lecture (and the brief question-answer period) with a workshop or seminar is a good way to deal in practical terms with the new material while its technical aspects are still fresh in everyone's mind.

Workshops and/or seminars frequently suffer from two common failures:

1. Groups are too large
2. Goals are not limited and defined

Workshop break-out groups should not exceed six or seven persons, and preferably should be limited to five. This will increase the likelihood of each individual's participation. Large groups tend to inhibit the members of the group who are the least aggressive in terms of expressing themselves before their peers. These individuals are sometimes your most thoughtfully incisive thinkers. If possible, then, keep the workshop group down to five, with random selection of group participants. Try to avoid buddying up at such sessions to avoid predictable results.

Any new product, new policy, or switch in company direction is complicated, and can lend itself to endless examination. It's your job to narrow down the discussion possibilities in a workshop to, at most, two key points. Any more than this will lead to diffuse, unfocused rap sessions rather than result-producing workshop conclusions.

For example, let's say you are introducing an entirely new packaging idea for one of your best-selling food products. The package is slightly larger than the current package, but the price of the unit remains the same.

This is an oversimplification, of course, but this brief summary of what's new already has sent both negative and positive waves of thought through the sales force. More for less? The customers will like that. Bigger package? The customers won't like that.

In this example, it probably would be a good idea to focus the workshops on how to overcome buyer objections to the size factor. Set aside considerations such as the appearance of the new package,

©Dartnell Corporation

use of color, type of container, etc. These will all arise in the discussion groups, but they should be secondary to thrashing out the focus question. It is up to each workshop leader, named by each group, to keep the group on track and, within a limited time, to present a summary of the group's recommendation on how to overcome the obvious buyer objection to a larger package.

Ask for five briefly stated methods of overcoming this objection and, to ensure that they are stated in brief, pass out a form similar to the one shown in Figure 1, below, to be filled in by the workshop leader at the end of the time allowed for discussion.

When you have these workshop responses in hand and have reviewed them, you will likely find a pattern of agreement in how best to approach the difficulties inherent in the merchandising of any new product development. What's more, your solutions will have been provided by those most immediately concerned, the salespeople.

Summarize and announce the workshop findings as soon as possible. If time permits, it is best to do this immediately following the workshop sessions and, in effect, to set an informal sales policy concerning the presentation of the new development.

Figure 1. Workshop Action Form

My group suggests the following techniques as the best methods to overcome buyer resistance to our new product:

1. _____
2. _____
3. _____
4. _____
5. _____

(Group leader)   (Date)

©Dartnell Corporation

Television, the friendly medium

Many sales managers are reluctant to use television at sales meetings, relying instead on the more traditional forms of equipment, such as slides, overhead transparencies and 16 mm. projectors. For members of several generations brought up with television, these traditional forms can be a bit dull.

Don't be afraid of TV. It's easy to hook up and is more trouble-free than most equipment. Most 16 mm. training films are now available on videocassette and are a lot easier than threading a projector. Consider the following advantages of television as a training tool.

1. *Television can be motivational.* It's well suited to showing the future and to painting a picture of achievement and success. Your salespeople are responsible for the continued jobs of your company's factory workers and service personnel. This can be dramatically demonstrated via television. Nothing is quite as motivational for people as seeing how they fit into the overall scheme of things.

2. *Television can stimulate discussion.* Use it to present a controversial issue or to get the audience emotionally involved. For example, if you're plagued by foreign competitors, you can use TV to show the benefits to our nation of buying U.S. goods, and evoke the nationalistic feelings it engenders. By dramatizing a specific event, with no conclusions drawn, you can turn off the set and let the discussion begin! Any conclusions or answers are provided by interaction among the learners themselves, through group discussion, role playing, or directed questions.

3. *Television can impart knowledge.* This will be particularly true when television is used to show the product or service in use. It can visually demonstrate the performance level expected. For example, your TV presentation can show a salesperson explaining the four major benefits of your new computerized ordering system. This is a good way to open a practice session.

4. *Television can teach sequential activities.* These might include such topics as five steps to the sale, how to prepare a telephone order, or how to assemble the new display rack. It's best to present the same sequence several times, preferably by different individuals. Follow this presentation by actual practice with your salespeople.

    In learning skills, whether cognitive, motor, or psychomotor, the repetition of responses is considered to be essential to the improvement of speed and proficiency. For example, television can be used:
    - To ask the student questions to test understanding
    - For drill practice, such as with the use of a personal computer
    - To direct the student to respond to workbook exercises
    - To respond orally to questions posed by the student
    - To respond interactively, via computer-assisted instruction
    - To test learner progress, using lifelike visual and spoken stimuli

    In the last example, the student is tested on his or her ability to respond appropriately to situations for which he or she is being trained, instead of being tested only on the ability to memorize. Because TV tests present real situations, they can avoid the ambiguities of meaning sometimes present in written or verbal tests. This results in greater test reliability.

5. *Television can present information in a variety of ways not possible with any other media.* Why? One reason is that considerably more effort is expended in developing a video production than would be expended in developing a classroom presentation.

    By presenting factual data on TV, the meeting leader is freed from the task of lesson preparation (at least partially) and to a great degree is released from the need to deliver long lectures and intricate presentations. Thus, the leader can devote his or her energies to other duties, such as observing behavior and counseling individual students.

These duties can be much more valuable than lecturing, particularly with an adult audience. The use of any media for the presentation of information will certainly enhance, rather than detract from, the value of a good trainer or meeting leader.

6. *Television can magnify and freeze any image.* It can blow-up a picture to hundreds or even thousands of times normal size. In recent years, there have been major improvements in big screen TV. Prices of this equipment have decreased, making it much more affordable. Most hotels and conference centers are able to obtain such equipment at a reasonable rental fee.

7. *Television, unlike film or slides, does not require the meeting room to be darkened.* This permits note-taking, allows for frequent stopping and starting of the videotape, and helps keep the audience alert during the presentation.

8. *Television can take the learner anywhere.* It can present a scene far away as well as one quite familiar to the audience—such as the inside of a supermarket. Television can build a bridge between theory and practice.

9. *Television has the advantage of being able to integrate most other audio-visual materials.* These might include a voice or sound, a still photograph or drawing, portions of a film, etc.

10. *Videotape playback is much easier than rewinding a film.* A videotape can be played back in a variety of ways to enhance learning. The repeated material might include:
    - A series of examples
    - A demonstration, such as how to use a new product
    - A series of steps in a procedure or process
    - Examples of one or more problems, followed by possible solutions

11. *Vocabulary problems may be overcome by saying and showing at the same time.* For example, "This is a stalactite, which always points downward and is formed by dripping from above. This is a stalagmite, a cylindrical or conical deposit,

projecting upward from the floor of a canyon." By superimposing the words on the picture and showing several shots, the learner should quickly learn the difference between the two and may even learn to spell the words!

12. *Television can be used for immediate feedback* when the television camera is in use, such as with role playing.

13. *The meeting leader or trainer can substantially reduce his or her preparation time* with televised instruction.

14. *Non-verbal information can be presented best through the television medium.* The audience is able to see facial expressions close-up, just like the real-life session in the buyer's office.

15. *No description by a meeting leader of what a salesperson did or said can come close to that action being replayed on the video screen.* The camera makes the judgment, not the leader or instructor. The instructor becomes a facilitator, not a judge.

16. *The cost of producing a videotape is far less than producing a film.* This is particularly advantageous when the presentation will be used only once or for a limited time. Additionally, time of preparation is far less for a video production.

17. Sesame Street *is proof positive that small children can learn new words faster and with more accuracy from television than from any other teaching process.* Why? Because the learner receives simultaneous signals through more than one sensory organ. The learner sees something and hears a voice talking about it, with a word or words superimposed on the bottom of the screen at the same time. In a classroom setting, the learning is further enhanced and reinforced by the meeting leader's words and, more particularly, by the discussion of the topic by the students themselves. This combination for learning is impossible to beat.

18. *Television allows the sales manager to bring subject matter experts and highly respected individuals to the sales meeting at a very small cost.* These individuals, such as the company president, leading educators, and other well known people

can talk to your sales force on a seemingly one-to-one basis. Via the tube, these individuals can explain, teach, and motivate your audience. They can do it over and over again, thanks to the long life of an inexpensive piece of videotape!

19. *Properly used, videotaped role playing can be one of the most valuable tools for any sales manager or sales trainer.* By working in small peer groups, with no threat of embarrassment, the television camera can teach a salesperson more than a dozen trips in the field would teach. Take the time to learn how to use and not misuse this powerful teaching tool.

20. *Television can present content in many forms, such as demonstration, group discussions, lecture, interviews, narration, voice-over, dramatic action, cartoons, graphics, etc.* By using different forms in a single presentation, you provide each student with one or more forms that appeal to him or her, that the student can identify with and is comfortable with. This point may be the most important thing to remember when you're developing a television program for your sales meeting: use more than one form!

Television should not be a budget-buster. It can be a budget-saver. If you do not own television equipment, it should be your next purchase. Buy an inexpensive camcorder for shots on the move. Buy the somewhat portable playback equipment. You can rent TV sets (monitors) inexpensively at most hotels. Conference centers have them built-in to most of their meeting rooms.

Why pay to fly your product managers and research people to your sales meetings? Capture them on videotape, edit the tape (removing corny stories and other trivia), and these individuals will look better on tape than in person.

Purchase camcorders for your salespeople and sales supervisors and ask them to bring on-the-job shots to the next sales meeting. Talk about *learning on the job!* Most of your people will work overtime to film the "best display" or "the biggest order" they've ever received. They will bring to the sales meeting an interview with the buyer(s)

©Dartnell Corporation

who made it all possible, explaining why they bought the "big order."

When used properly, the friendly medium of television will give your sales meeting the professional touch, along with a very high return on your investment.

Film

A word of caution here is advisable. Films (and video) can be the lazy man's or woman's way out in building training into sales meetings. Simply put, there are films and then there are films. It's time-wasting and even counter-productive to use film and video in training, unless what is being shown is pertinent to the product or to your firm.

It well may be that a picture is worth a thousand words, but not if the picture has nothing to do, except in a remote way, with what you are trying to explain.

How many sales meetings have you attended in which, for example, a generalized sales techniques film is played, supposedly to stir enthusiasm? Probably far too many. The market abounds in such films and, at this very moment, doubtless many are in production and being played to hapless assemblages of salespeople.

If you are fortunate enough to have the resources to produce your own specific training film or video, you possess a potent training tool. If not, be prepared to pre-screen all generalized market offerings before booking them for your sales meetings. This is about the only method to use to ensure you don't end up with a clinker, or one that has little or no informative value to your group.

It is all-important, if you are buying stock footages, to review them in person, or to book them only when you have the opinion of a trusted colleague. Here, too, watch out for the overly impersonal instructional film.

Role playing

What this amounts to is setting up mini-dramas pertinent to a sales situation and then asking your salespeople to enact the various roles in the drama.

No one need be an actor to participate and it is better if no one is, but each person in the mini-drama should take his or her role seriously. The ideal is to keep role play on as serious a level as possible, and to make sure that the "plot" is germane to the sales situation involved. Avoid outlandish situations or ones that might produce humor but little substance. Be sure you keep the cast in these mini-dramas down to a miminum.

To set the scene for role play, it is necessary to make some hard choices about the structure of the plot of the mini-drama. The key here is to *be specific*. Don't allow room for rambling observations in the spontaneous dialogue. Stick to one single issue.

Your plots to be played out by the salespeople have one aim: training by example. They also should be realistic, representing something that any of the staff would be likely to encounter in his or her daily rounds.

Let's say your firm is undergoing a radical change in packaging, complete with new logo. One possible scenario would be to have a sales rep explaining why the change will be of benefit to his or her customer, a role assigned to another salesperson. They might just happen to be sitting with the buyer's boss, a tough merchandising manager. That's the bare bones of your plot, and your actors can take it from there within a set time frame.

Allow the actors to play their roles with no interruptions. Then call for an open critique of how the objections were met, how the change was explained as an advantage to buyer and consumer, and how the buyer's objections were framed (realistic, logical, or just plain ornery).

This critique session is a valuable part of the role-play process, because invariably the audience was thinking of a number of points to make while the mini-drama was unfolding. This is the time when all these points will come forth.

In role play it is essential to avoid any embarrassment to anyone. Some people think faster on their feet, while others are more reflective. Listening to role play—and participating in the critique that follows—can be particularly valuable to those on your staff who tend to be more introverted than others. It is therefore important to call on as many reps as possible during the critique session following the dramatic presentation.

©Dartnell Corporation

The give-and-take that normally follows a role-play session may give you some worries about staying on schedule with the meeting. Keep in mind that role play generally is very absorbing to sales personnel. It is therefore one of the most valuable methods of building training into your meeting.

Evaluating training effectiveness

A time arrives, usually at the end of the meeting, when you must face the unavoidable question, "Was the meeting effective?" There are a wide variety of possible evaluation procedures, any or all of which might give you the clues you need to assess the effectiveness of the meeting honestly.

The quiz

The evaluation quiz is much like the surprise quiz we have all faced in school. The trick is to make the quiz pertinent but not tricky. The best method to use is multiple choice; the next best is true or false. The least effective is the essay-answer quiz.

You are trying to find out how much of the training has sunk in. If very little has, you have your answer about the effectiveness of the meeting. The converse also is true.

Any quiz should be prepared in advance and should be as uncomplicated in format as possible. Pass it out at the end of a training session and give a time limit for its conclusion. Don't make your questions deliberately tricky or ambiguous.

A sample quiz appears in Figure 2 on page 68.

Note that each suggested question asks something specific and offers a specific answer. Anticipated answers should all be reasonable and in line with what has been discussed during the training session.

Audience participation

Audience participation, or review of the material covered, necessitates that you act as the questioner and call at random on individuals in the audience for responses. In a sense, this amounts to an oral quiz and is perhaps the fastest way to determine if the training session was productive.

Audience participation, aside from speedy feedback, offers the advantage of correcting mistaken or incorrect views on the spot. In dealing with such matters as commission rates, company car policies,

Figure 2. Sample Sales Training Quiz

1. The new product will be first introduced
   - ☐ in two markets
   - ☐ nationwide
   - ☐ in metro Chicago area
2. Test marketing has shown a possible
   - ☐ 10 percent sales increase potential
   - ☐ 30 percent possible increase in shelf space
   - ☐ cannibalism of our brand X
3. Shipping of new product will be from
   - ☐ Omaha factory
   - ☐ Salt Lake City warehouse
   - ☐ jobber network being established
4. Main advantage of new packaging is
   - ☐ sight impact
   - ☐ use of the word "new" in bold above name
   - ☐ pouring convenience for consumer
5. Commission rate on new product for first year will be
   - ☐ same as for other products
   - ☐ based on 5 percent net if 100 new accounts opened
   - ☐ worked out as we continue test marketing
6. The main objection I may encounter is
   - ☐ new size of package
   - ☐ delivery distance
   - ☐ cutback on co-op advertising

©Dartnell Corporation

etc., audience participation is invaluable as a technique of learning how well the sales meeting "took" with the sales personnel. It is a way, too, to avoid misunderstandings that can fester into major morale problems if not corrected when everyone is together.

Small group discussion

Small group discussion can be a valuable tool to use in assessing meeting effectiveness. This can be either structured or free-flowing. The valuable part of this technique becomes apparent if you remember playing that old parlor game in which you turn to the person on your right and whisper a story to him or her. That person repeats the story to the next person and so on, with the last person in the ring telling the story aloud. The story, as you know, will turn out to be radically different from the one you first told.

Discussion of a situation by small groups tends to cut down on future misunderstandings. In effect, it cuts down the risk factor inherent in the truism that people tend to hear what they want to hear.

In small group discussions it is important that you, and other experts you have had on the training program, be on hand to clear up anything that may arise out of these sessions. Following small group discussions, it is a good idea for you to review, once again, the major points made during the training session. Learning, particularly if the subject is difficult, is accomplished by repeated review, or practice with the facts.

However, not too much time should be devoted to these small group discussions. If they drag on, the tendency is for them to become exercises in futility. Keep them brief and, while they are going on, circulate as much as possible to see that they stay on track and, more importantly, to pick up on where the problem areas may be.

Written evaluations

Another way to measure how effective the training sessions were is to ask for written evaluations. It is best in this to 1) limit the scope of the essay and 2) make the question as general as possible. As a rule, the written evaluation as applied to training effectiveness is not too effective. It does, however, have one major advantage: it cements in a person's mind a major point by requiring that person to write it down. In other words, it encourages thought.

©Dartnell Corporation

Observation

When the session is finished, observe the mood in the room. This is called the happiness quotient, and, while not totally reliable (the people might just be happy because they are going home), the mood of the participants is a good indicator of how much the salespeople got from the meeting.

There is no question that the vast majority of your salespeople are intelligent, hard-working individuals who are eager for education in the products or services they sell for a living. If they have learned something at the meeting about how to improve their incomes, that's reason enough for joy. However, there's more to it than that. Everyone likes to be part of a go-go organization, one that takes itself and its reputation seriously. Knowledge is power. Unfortunately now a cliché, this statement is nonetheless valid. Your salespeople know this. The more knowledge they've packed away at the sales meeting, the happier they will be. It's pervasive, too. You can't help but notice the mood at the conclusion of a meeting.

If it's happy at the end, you've succeeded in your training efforts; if it's downbeat, you'll know something went awry, probably a failure to build the right kind of training into your meeting.

Section 8

Special Types of Sales Meetings

Most established firms, whatever their size or sales volume, have fairly standard procedures governing the frequency and location of their sales meetings. In many industries, the sales meeting is a direct outgrowth of market traditions. The sales meeting can be semi-annual, as in much of the soft goods industry, or annual, as in the case of much of heavy industry.

Sales meetings have logically focused on products to introduce to the sales force, which is probably the single most impelling reason to hold a meeting.

In addition to these market-induced gatherings, there are a wide variety of special sales meetings, those which fit no particular pattern dictated by market tradition.

A new twist, too, on the incidence of these special meetings has emerged in recent years, brought on by the rash of mergers and acquisitions in corporate America. Frequently these mergers bring with them entirely new approaches to product merchandising, elimination of some product lines, and, not infrequently, corporate name changes. Several of the company logos all of us thought were cast in concrete have been nevertheless replaced by new acronyms.

These mergers often affect large sales forces, sometimes negatively in terms of lost jobs. Whatever the effects in human terms, the mergers themselves call for orientation of combined sales organizations and, of course, education in a whole new set of operating policies and procedures. It's much like starting over for many sales professionals these days.

©Dartnell Corporation

The nationwide "big special"

Thus, at this moment in history, one of the most common special meetings is the one that is a direct outgrowth of a mighty financial transaction at investment banking boardrooms. This type of special meeting is a close relative to the old-time nationwide meeting called for some unique purpose, such as the yearly message from the chairman and/or chief executive officer.

There are special problems, of course, in organizing the nationwide meeting, whether it comes about because of merger-mania or because of some important development within the structure of an independent firm. The main problem in such a meeting—that of getting it off the ground—centers on logistics, an imposing task for any meeting organizer.

Special meetings on a nationwide, company-wide basis can involve hundreds and even thousands of people, although the trend has been to hold down the numbers as much as possible and break out the details at regional gatherings following the big event.

In any event, organizing a nationwide gathering is a formidable task and an expensive one.

Location of such a meeting is the first consideration. Because of the number of people involved, the meeting must be held in as central a location as possible. It also should be held in a large city, since the number of rooms needed may preclude using smaller communities. Nationwide specials invariably attract the big guns in any organization, so the meeting location frequently must be built around the desires of the very top management people.

Often, the lead time for the big special meeting is not as favorable as the organizer would like, which is all the more reason to choose a large city for the meeting. You stand a better chance of getting what you want (and fast) from a large hotel or convention site.

Along with picking and nailing down the meeting site, you face another logistical problem in transportation. This is an additional reason to pick a large, centralized city, preferably one that is a hub of a major airline. Here is where a good relationship with a travel agency will prove invaluable. If you do enough business with the

©Dartnell Corporation

agency on a continuing basis, it is a good idea to turn over to them all travel arrangements for the meeting.

Because most large hotels and convention sites are used to crisis management of one sort or another, it is a good idea to have the hotel staff assist you with detailed planning, once you have supplied attendance figures, meals required, meeting rooms needed, and back-up services necessary. The same forms shown in Section 3 for organizing a smaller, less hectic meeting will be useful in assembling the necessary data.

After coping with logistics, the next problem is to figure out a program applicable to such an obviously diverse group of people, many of whom have never met one another and who have little in common except that they work for the same firm. The primary goal of the big special, generally, is informational—to get across key developments within the firm to top people so that these can be passed on and digested at smaller, less formal regional gatherings. Except in rare circumstances, there is not enough time at a big special to deal with traditional sales meeting goals and objectives.

The big special concentrates on broad policy issues, followed, if possible, by discussion of how these policies are to be implemented. There probably will not be time, or even space, to break off into workshop groups or seminars to hash out traditional sales problems.

It is a good idea to videotape this major gathering for use later in regional meetings. This is particularly important if the chief executive officer or chairman in an acquisition or merger situation explains just what went on and what lies ahead. Use of a videotape of what actually was said by the boss will go a long way in alleviating doubts and uncertainties on the part of the sales force. Use of videotape when a major new product is introduced at a big special also will be reassuring to all salespeople before they actually get a hands-on feel for the introduction.

Planning the program for a nationwide gathering is critical because a great deal of material usually must be crammed into a limited time. This is best accomplished by focusing on policy issues, keynoted by top brass, and on how to implement the policies formulated.

The meeting announcing a new business or subsidiary

Another type of special meeting is the one that has to do with the opening of a new business, or a subsidiary. Here the logistics depend on the size of the gathering, but the same rules of using checklists and keeping a handle on accounting matters apply.

Because everything and everyone is unfamiliar, this type of sales meeting poses a special problem in regard to making good first impressions. Therefore, it is your task to formulate a program that will fire up the sales force and quickly establish the reason for the firm and its products to compete in the marketplace. This is no small task and requires considerable advance planning.

If the product is brand new or highly unusual, your task will be to establish its need. If the product is competitive, how can you establish a need for it except by its lower pricing? Price reduction is the easy way out, but one that many rely on excessively at opening sales meetings. Search long and hard for other competitive advantages before relying on price at the introductory sales meeting.

Your first-time meeting will require devoting more time than usual to explaining nitty-gritty company policies. These may include everything from delivery practices to methods of compensation. It is critical at such a gathering to have printed and ready for distribution a complete and readable employee manual; it is equally important to go over this manual step by step, clearing up any questions as they arise during the discussion. Don't fall into the trap at this crucial time of saying, "We can talk about that later." Talk about it at the beginning and clear up each point as it arises. This part of the meeting should also be attended by key support personnel, such as the head of the delivery section, the comptroller, the ad manager, etc. This will be reassuring not only to the sales force, but to the department heads themselves. It is important to create a team approach right from the beginning, even if this procedure might take up what you consider time needed for discussion of sales techniques.

©Dartnell Corporation

Special Types of Sales Meetings 75

Other special meetings

There are a number of other occasions for special meetings, all with different formats and objectives. Descriptions of some of these types of meetings follow.

New product introductions

Due to increasing competition, even the most hidebound industries are introducing new products when they are ready to go and not waiting until the annual or semi-annual sales gatherings.

These meetings are in a sense the easiest and sometimes the most rewarding to organize and bring off. They are relatively easy because the meeting has a direct focus—a new product or service; and they are rewarding because newness—if the product or service really is new—is intrinsically exciting to everyone, particularly to a sales force.

The task is to *sell* the new product or service to your own people. It may be a product that competes directly with one of your firm's established favorites; or it may be a product with consumer appeal, but bulky or difficult to show. Sometimes a new product may even pose a threat to the salespeople, who are more comfortable with what they are selling at the moment.

One of the best techniques to use in selling your own people a new product is to step aside and turn the platform over to the people who came up with and implemented the idea. These people, be they stylists, packaging experts, or inventors, frequently speak with great sincerity (after all, it's their baby!), even if they may not visualize the product's sales potential in your terms. Allow these experts to be questioned at whatever length and allow them, in their own words, to outline the product's advantages. You may not convince every salesperson in the room by this technique, but you are almost certain to gain allies from the most skilled salespeople. Another advantage in letting the experts speak is that a perceptive salesperson invariably will pick up sales pointers from such a presentation, pointers that he or she later can translate into benefits for a buyer.

Telephone conference calls

This type of meeting has, in recent years, been in vogue and has yet to realize its full potential. That's because too many have expected too much from it and have viewed the technique as a way to save

©Dartnell Corporation

both time and money. However, although the telephone conference call does both, it can be counter-productive to sales achievement when not used appropriately.

The biggest single misuse of the technique seems to be the temptation to cram too much into the session. It can become woefully hit and miss without stern format procedures, so focus on one or two items for discussion. The technology in most hands simply does not lend itself to a full-blown meeting.

Telephone conference calls have been, however, highly successful in tackling specific sales problems, such as closing the sale, or line presentation. The trick seems to be to zero in on one subject, then stick to the subject for a relatively brief time. Long telephone sessions, which can be costly, also can be boring in the extreme. The reason is simple: the impersonal nature of the technique removes the interpersonal excitement of true communication, which is to say the nuance factor involved in observing another person's face while speaking. Nevertheless, for single-subject problems it is a valuable tool and one that can indeed save you money.

Meetings for contest winners

This type of meeting has taken a needlessly bad rap in recent days, probably because there's a bit of jealousy among the non-winners, or some resentment among the winners in having to attend a meeting as penance of sorts for being a winner. Neither position is justified if such a meeting is structured to do what it is supposed to do: improve on excellence.

If such a meeting is no more than an extended trip to a spa, with little but socializing involved, it probably will create jealousy. If it's a long haul over familiar territory, it will induce boredom. What is the happy medium at a meeting of contest winners?

In coming to grips with this dilemma, it is a good idea to keep foremost in mind that the reason you have assembled these people is because they are good—and people who are good generally want to be even better. That's an oversimplification, but think it through. People get to be good because they are always learning.

It follows, then, that a meeting of contest winners should focus on shared experiences, and should function as an enlarged rap session dealing with sales techniques. Be certain to set aside time to praise and to hand out awards.

Role playing is an excellent means of focusing on sales techniques. Sometimes the best on your staff don't know how good they may be at certain sales techniques. Devise scenarios for the role playing to attempt to bring out little tricks of the trade. Then tape record the actual sessions, editing and using the results later, without naming names, for general meetings.

What should be avoided at such meetings are nuts-and-bolts reviews of company policy and any references to the possible shortcomings of colleagues not fortunate enough to have won a contest.

Tele-conferencing

This is a fine technique for attacking an immediate problem. It is no substitute, of course, for a general discussion of the problem. But teleconferencing between sales gatherings can get a lot of troublesome items out of the way in a hurry. The trouble with the technique in too many cases is that teleconferencing can turn into tele-lecturing. To avoid this, have a specific agenda (small) before plugging in, follow it carefully, and establish a dialogue on a specific issue. Then reach a conclusion for action. Too many teleconferences dwindle off into the sunset with, "Well, okay, nice to get your views, and I'll be talking to you." Go into a teleconference with the idea that a plan of action will result or that you will impart some vital information clearly and explicitly.

The gripe session

The following types of meetings are valuable if they are not prolonged and if they focus on, at most, two points.

The most common is the gripe session which, handled in an up-front manner, can be more productive than it sounds. Everyone occasionally needs to get something off his or her chest, and griping to the boss (who should know how to listen) is a healthy way to open the steam valve. These sessions are no good if confidentiality is not assured. All you'll get will be mild tap-dancing around a problem if recrimination is feared. Make it clear that frankness is respected—and required. Make sure you take notes during the session, which you should later transcribe and act on, or at least respond to. It is best in a gripe session to avoid confrontation or argument. After all, you essentially hold the cards. Listen, then act, and maintain confidentiality. You'll soon learn who the born complainers are. Hearing from the others makes it worth listening to these few.

The boasting session

Sometimes the opposite of the gripe session is in order, too. This is the boasting session, which is just what the name implies, especially if you have a congenial group. Here's when success stories flow like fine wine, and with much the same intoxicating effect. Psychologically, the gripe and boasting sessions accomplish much the same thing. They provide an emotional safety valve and personalize what sometimes can be the dust-dry routines of an average salesperson's day. Best of all, they buttress one's sense of self-worth, and, minimizing the tendency to exaggeration, boasting sessions actually can focus on techniques that have proven successful and should be shared.

The case study session

A more serious type of special meeting is the one involving the use of case studies. These are highly productive if—and it's a big if—the studies are well documented and have a beginning, a middle, and an end. These are narratives of a specific sales encounter, including what happened and perhaps why it happened. They can be either success stories or admitted failures. That's not important. What is important is that they provide guidelines for use by other members of the staff. Be sure you allow plenty of time for case study preparation when you call such a meeting, and offer general formats for preparing a case study. It is important in this type of meeting to allow enough time for presentation of a case study, but not too much time for introspection on the part of its author. Just tell it as it was. Then allot a fixed time for questions and comments. Case study meetings also should never have more than five or six participants per break-off group, and preferably those with similar sales problems or territories.

Section 9

Workshops and Seminars

Since the ultimate aim of any sales gathering can be summed up by the word *education*, two of the most popular—and valid—techniques to achieve this goal are workshops and seminars. Differing only in degree and format, each aims to educate the sales force.

A workshop can be defined, simply, as learning by doing, which is usually the most efficient way of learning. A seminar, with the same aim, is structured differently in that a seminar is led by an expert in the topic under discussion. This expert guides the flow of the session.

Both the workshop and the seminar can be used with good results within the framework of a full-scale meeting or convention, or both can stand alone as mini or ad hoc sales meetings. In other words, both are good techniques to employ for the continuing education of salespeople.

As mentioned before, the current and ongoing crop of sales professionals put greater stress on education than their peers of earlier generations. It no longer is enough to achieve success in sales with a good personality or by dint of hard work (although these two qualities help a lot). Now the need is for product knowledge, sound psychological insight, and time management. Again, your most successful salespeople these days are those who are always learning and who admit they still have a lot to learn. Knowledge is power when it comes to sales performance. You don't have to articulate that to your brighter young people. They know it without being told, which is why effective workshops and seminars at sales meetings generally are the most popular and well-attended items on the agenda.

©Dartnell Corporation

In using either workshops or seminars within the framework of a sales meeting, it is important to make sure that they have a relevancy to the overall meeting, or to the theme of the meeting itself. Don't throw a workshop into the program as an afterthought; ideally it should follow closely on the heels of a generalized presentation, such as the introduction of a new line.

The workshop (or seminar) should have a definite time limit since a deadline for the individual groups forces incisive thinking and decision making.

The workshop

Generally, a workshop should consume no more than an hour or two of your schedule and should be structured by breaking your group down into sections of from five to fifteen people. Round tables to accommodate each section should be available, along with pencils and writing pads. One person selected by the group functions as chairperson and another should serve as recorder of what is said.

As an example, if the workshops are to focus on current pricing objections in the market, the chairperson should state the problem (all groups should have the same problem on the table), then go around the table person by person, asking for comments and possible ideas on how to overcome the problem. Everyone in a group should have the opportunity to analyze the problem and to offer a solution or even a variety of solutions. When this round-robin is completed, the recorder will read back what has been said and the floor then opens for general discussion of solutions. Since everyone is involved in this process, chances are the discussion period will be lively. It is the responsibility of the chairperson to keep things moving and to avoid repetition.

At some point a consensus very likely will be reached; from this consensus, the group prepares a report. If there is a disagreement right up to the end, a minority report may be called for.

It is a good idea, if you can afford it, to have various experts from within the company, or even from outside, circulating among the groups to offer technical assistance (i.e., why the new product has to cost more than the one it will be replacing).

©Dartnell Corporation

When the time limit is up for the workshops, the reports are handed in and the conclusions read to the entire group; or, each group may give its own report. You'll very likely be startled at the general agreement on how best to solve a particular problem. This group interaction therefore sets the guidelines on how the firm and individual salespeople will attempt to solve the problem.

A variation of the workshop idea that is viable for very large conventions or meetings is to name a committee from within the entire group to thrash out the problem and make a report. But this technique is best used only when time limitations on group workshops are severe.

How does a seminar differ from a workshop?

The seminar, while its aim is much the same as the workshop, is normally more tightly structured. A seminar ideally should be composed of people who already have considerable knowledge of a situation and who are looking to gain more knowledge and then pass it on.

A seminar leader should be an expert in the area under discussion. He or she conducts the session, lays out the factors involved in the equation, and then solicits general discussion on possible solutions to the problem. A workshop has some of the elements of a buzz session; a seminar is an attempt to push knowledge a step further with expert testimony and guidance.

When to use a workshop

One of the best times to use either a seminar or workshop format is when you are attempting to define a touchy issue.

Maybe, as an example, you have been arguing with your boss about a particularly touchy pricing issue. He probably remarks to you, "Well, what will our people think of this? I'd like to know." That's the time for a workshop, which is the fastest method of finding out the reactions of salespeople. Workshops will also educate the staff on the reasons for the pricing changes and perhaps even on the necessity for them. Best of all, the interplay during the workshops will generally bring out solid methods of how to cope with the new situation, or at least how to make it more palatable. Workshop conclusions also frequently result in functional compromises. Everyone becomes part of a major decision. What's more, the boss invariably finds out what he asked of you, i.e., "What will our people think?"

Workshops and seminars also are valuable as educational tools when the company is introducing a new co-op ad program, a new group of dealers' aids, a new commission schedule, a new pension or benefits program, or territory realignments. The list could go on. A workshop format is ideal to further the understanding of a shift in any direction within the company. In addition to the valuable educational aspects involved, the workshops also will cut down in many cases on a lot of negative scuttlebutt within the company when a new direction is introduced.

Workshops are equally valuable in tackling specific sales problems: how to show a complicated new product; how to broaden a distribution base within territories; how to explain a new discount policy.

Importance of context

The things to remember in using the workshop or seminar format are to be specific in your choice of topics and *make sure they are in context with the rest of the meeting.* A broad-gauged workshop topic can and probably will produce a lot of good conversation, but it will also offer few conclusions.

Another good thing about the workshop format is the ease it offers in getting good participation and involvement. In fact, in a large meeting or convention, it may be the only means you can come up with to give everyone a chance to get in his or her two cents' worth.

It is, of course, up to the chairperson of the workshop or seminar to make sure everyone sounds off. In the workshop, however, participation is obligatory. You literally are called upon to offer views. The seminar chairperson will have to be more careful to get complete participation, particularly among the more reticent or introverted individuals on the staff. He or she should make sure that each person at least has a chance to speak to the problem.

It is never a good idea to spring surprise problems on a workshop group. Instead, before the group breaks down into workshop units, you should make it crystal clear what the problem or topic is. Avoid reverse type topics, those that start out with, "But on the other hand, if . . ."

Frame the workshop question in simple declarative terms: "Here's the problem. Now what should we do about it?" This avoids tricky or clever solutions and avoids wasting a lot of time in the workshop sessions themselves.

Workshop ideas

Use seminars or workshops at your sales meeting to:
1. Teach product knowledge
2. Teach selling skills
3. Create greater interest in a product or service
4. Gain understanding of a market, customer, or customer type
5. Cross-train sales forces
6. Build enthusiasm
7. Gain insight
8. Collect ideas

Here are a few examples:

Different type customer

You are asking your salespeople to call on dentists as well as medical doctors. There are certain things that dentists do differently, and their interest in your particular medications is slightly different. You could simply tell your salespeople the differences, but they will remember better and you will appear more believable if they have an opportunity to discuss it among themselves first.

Start by asking small break-off groups to identify what they believe the differences to be. Give them ten minutes or so to come up with their conclusions. Then assemble the groups and compare notes. Put on the board all the reasons given. Then, alongside each reason, put your own notes indicating what research information says on the subject.

Finally, break the groups again with the assignment, "As a result of these differences, how should the dentists be approached?" Again, give the groups ten or fifteen minutes to arrive at their conclusions before bringing them together for a review of each group's finding, followed by a question and answer session.

©Dartnell Corporation

New product or product line

Following a presentation of the product to the entire gathering, break-off groups can address a number of problems and opportunities. Pick what you believe to be the greatest area of opportunity and start with that, having everyone work on it in small groups.

For example, you've selected getting shelf space as the biggest single problem that your new cigarette brand will have. The break-off groups can work on the problem and come up with a number of possible solutions.

Another approach would be to have the entire group develop a laundry list of potential problems with the introduction of the new cigarette brand. The list can then be put in priority order by the entire group. Once this is done, give each small work group one priority item to resolve. Then bring the groups back together to hear a report from each group.

Demonstrating a new product

Your new weed-whacker works better and faster and is safer to use, but also requires more knowledge to demonstrate to a prospective customer. What should you do?

First, you can show the new features by means of slides or videotape and/or you can show the actual weed-whacker assembled and disassembled. This will provide an overview of the features and benefits and may also show the equipment in action.

However, being able to demonstrate this little jewel is another matter. First the salespeople must learn how to get it running! Hands-on training is the best solution. Rather than have the entire group take turns, provide one new weed-whacker for every two or three salespeople and have them work together practicing the demonstration.

At this point you can have one or more subject matter experts go from one group to another helping and answering questions, or you can have each group alone figure things out for themselves. In any case, you'll want to pull the entire group back together to compare notes. To have a little fun, you can award one or more prizes for the best demonstrations, the judging being done, of course, by the salespeople themselves.

©Dartnell Corporation

Finish the workshop with an open discussion of the product and the product demonstration.

Building a presentation

This is a variation of brainstorming. Let's consider a situation where the closing ratio of your sales force on a particular product is very poor. Your goal at this sales meeting is to have your people develop from scratch a powerful verbal presentation that will substantially increase the closing ratio.

If your total group is small, say 20 persons or fewer, there's no need to split them up. Place three or four flip charts at the front of the room. Station a fast writer at each, with felt-tip markers in hand.

Explain that the group will build a presentation on the spot. Start by asking for opening words or statements. Keep them short. Write down as many as are offered. Anyone can call them out, and the more the better. When you've exhausted the audience of ideas for the opening statement, pull all the sheets off the flip charts and tape them to the walls. You may have 20 to 50 ideas.

Then move on to the body of the presentation and repeat the steps noted above, taping them to another wall of your meeting room. Finally, work on the closing statement, following the same procedure. Now you have the walls covered with statements.

Now comes the best part of this exercise. You return to the wall of opening statements and have the assembled groups determine which is the most powerful. This can be done by putting them in priority order or simply by asking the group to rate each on a scale of one to ten. Whatever procedure you use, you will end up with three or four dynamite openings that most everyone agrees with.

Next, repeat the procedure for the body of the presentation and the closing. After all that work, you're left with three, four, or five openings, three, four, or five central bodies of presentation, and similar numbers of closing statements.

"Is it worth all that work?" you ask. "Why not simply hand out presentations prepared by the sales manager or sales training manager?" Yes, it is worth the time and work, because now you have

©Dartnell Corporation

something that your salespeople developed for *themselves.* They own it! If they try it out and it doesn't work, who are they to blame?

If, after the exercises noted above are complete, you still have time, you can again break off into small groups of three or four to practice using the ideas your people have generated.

Knowing your customer

Here's an exercise that will not only get your salespeople to think about what customer information they need, but will also teach them how to use it.

Open the session by explaining what you plan to do and how each person will benefit from the exercises. Tell the group that any good salesperson will have considerable knowledge about a customer and about the customer's personnel. The secret, you explain, is finding out the few important things that you can use to improve your business with a particular account. The question really becomes, "What specific information, if I had it, would significantly increase my ability to accomplish my goals with this account?"

Once they understand the ground rules, continue as follows:

1. Ask each salesperson to write down the names of their three most important customers.
2. Ask each salesperson to select one customer from the three that, if certain information could be obtained, would be most beneficial to the salesperson and the company.
3. Now that each person in the audience has selected one account, ask him or her to write, in priority order, the top three pieces of missing information about that account. If time allows, you could have longer lists, but three is a good number.
4. Break off into groups of three or four, asking each person to help the others in his or her group come up with at least one new way to obtain the missing information.
5. Bring everyone back together to find out what happened. Ask several groups to read off the missing information and the suggestions on how it might be obtained.
6. If time allows, you can ask each person to write the three missing pieces of information on the top portion of a sheet of

chart paper and tape each one on the wall of the meeting room. Then ask each person to walk around, read a chart, and write their suggestion on the lower portion of the chart paper. When you're through, each person can retrieve his or her own sheet and take it home. This part of the exercise works best when you can leave the charts up for several days.

7. The final portion of this exercise, if you choose to do it, is the actual practice of asking for the information. This can best be handled by role play, with some input from the sales manager or meeting leader as to how the information can be most easily obtained. A key point to make is that a straightforward request for the information from the customer or prospect is sometimes the best and is certainly the easiest approach.

The "grinder"

The "grinder," developed by Ray Higgins, Director, Sales Training & Development, The Dial Corporation, is a training procedure that can be used when you want your salespeople to get a lot of practice in a short period of time.

It is role playing done quickly, with a constantly changing customer or prospect. It works best when you want your sales force to be able to answer a specific question or handle an objection that occurs frequently. Here's an example. Your company has just brought out a fourth size of your miracle laundry detergent. The box is so large that it has wheels and a handle. The test markets have determined that the product moves well, but getting the grocer to stock it initially has been difficult. His complaint is, "It won't fit on the shelf. Where can I display it?"

The company has determined that there are several ideal locations for the product, but they may not be acceptable to some store managers. What the salespeople need is not only to learn about many possible responses to the question, "Where can I display it?" but they also need practice in discussing it with their customers.

The "grinder" comes to the rescue! Take the total number of salespeople in your meeting and place the same number of chairs in the back of your meeting room or in another room (use an even number). Divide the chairs into two equal rows, facing each other, with about two feet of space between the chairs in the same row. Leave only enough room between the facing chairs so that individuals can comfortably sit without their knees touching one another. The chairs will look like those shown in Figure 1, below.

Figure 1. Chair Arrangement for the "Grinder"

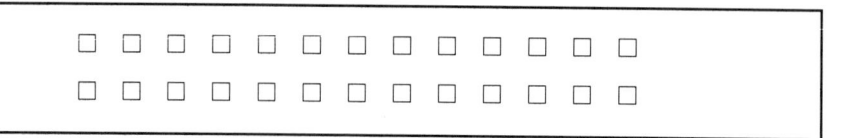

Next have everyone select a chair and sit down. Then advise those in one row that they will be customers and those in the other row that they will be salespeople. Instruct the customers to say only one thing to start: "Where can I display it?" When the person sitting directly across from them answers, they are free to say anything they like and to play the customer role as they see fit.

All this sounds vaguely familiar, but wait! There's a catch! When you blow your whistle, every pair starts talking, but they have only one minute until you blow the whistle again and all conversation must stop. After the first minute, ask each salesperson to move down one chair, with the one on the end moving to the chair on the far end. The customers stay where they are. You blow the whistle again and let them talk for a minute. You continue to change partners until each salesperson has talked with each customer. Now have the groups switch chairs, with the salespeople becoming customers and vice versa. Repeat the entire process again.

Not only is this exercise a lot of fun, it is non-threatening, allowing each of your salespeople to be exposed to one or more ideas from each of their peers. When you've completed the "grinder," bring the entire group back together to talk about their experience and to vote on who was the best customer and who was the best salesperson.

The quiz bowl This exercise is valuable when you want your salespeople to remember certain key facts or information. It's especially useful when you're introducing a new product or service.

©Dartnell Corporation

Prior to your sales meeting, make a list of the key information, such as price, terms, top three features, etc. When you've finished, you should have 25 to 50 specific pieces of information that you feel are important. Take each one and place it on a 3 x 5 card, in the form of a question, i.e., What is the suggested retail price of our new deluxe pen and pencil set? What are the two side-effects of our new drug for allergy relief? and so on. Leave the answers off, but attach a fresh, new one-dollar bill to the back of each card.

Next, be sure that all the answers to the questions on the cards have been given to the sales force during the meeting in one form or another, but don't tell anyone about the Quiz Bowl. At the end of the day, or near the end of the meeting, have everyone draw their chairs in a circle and place all the cards in a big fish bowl or similar container. Place the bowl in the middle of the circle.

Advise everyone that this is a contest and that if the person choosing a card can answer the question, he or she can keep the dollar. However, if he or she cannot answer or answers incorrectly, the individual must pass the card to the person seated next to him, adding a dollar of his or her own to the card. The next person gets a chance to answer and, if he or she answers correctly, may keep the two dollars. If he or she fails, the non-respondent must add another dollar and pass the card along. When the correct answer is given, the next person selects a new card and the game continues. The game will be a lot of fun for everyone and provides reinforcement learning on the key items that you want everyone to remember.

Work plan example

You don't need to be a professional teacher or trainer to develop and conduct a workshop or seminar for your salespeople. All you need is an idea and a little preparation time. Shown in Figure 2, page 90, is an actual work plan that I developed for a group of writing instrument salespeople on the topic of product knowledge. Please notice that the main points of my presentation/discussion were contained on overhead transparencies. This made it easier for me to remember what came next and also provided material for discussion.

**Figure 2.
Detailed
Work Plan**

Topic:	Product Knowledge
Time:	30 Minutes
Design:	Lecture/Discussion
	Use overhead projector

Once complete, the work plan becomes your notes when teaching the class.

Open by making the point that product knowledge by itself is useless. Ask for someone in the audience who has recently purchased a new car. Then put up the following transparency and fill in the blanks as he or she answers the question.

Transparency #1

Make of car_____
Model_____
Cylinders_____
Bore_____inches
Stroke_____inches
Compression ratio_____
Horsepower_____
Wheelbase_____
Track_____
Body length_____
Body width_____
Weight (dry)_____
Fuel tank_____gallons

Then make the point that the car salesperson probably quoted some of these statistics when selling the car, but, if a good salesperson, did it to prove other points of greater interest to the buyer.

I use this example to make a key point about product knowledge. This is the first of five laws of product knowledge that I want you to remember. Since I thought them up, let's call them "Rapp's 5 Laws of Product Knowledge."

©Dartnell Corporation

Transparency #2   Rapp's Law #1: It is not having it that is important, it is knowing how to use it.

That's pretty straightforward, so let's move quickly to Law #2.

Transparency #3   Rapp's Law #2: P.K. x G.S. = Cs and Cc.

Translation: Product knowledge in the hand of a good salesperson equals confidence for the salesperson, which in turn produces confidence in the customer.

This is sometimes overlooked, but the greatest asset any salesperson has is the confidence and trust that the customer places in the salesperson.

Of course we should not overlook the traditional benefits of product knowledge, which are to:

- Explain features and benefits
- Answer questions
- Fit products to customer needs
- Handle complaints

In line with these traditional reasons for product knowledge, we come to Transparency #4.

Transparency #4   Rapp's Law #3: Always Put the Cart Before the Horse.

Liberally translated, this means that you should first determine the special needs/interest (the cart) of the customer, before you start spewing forth your product knowledge (the horse). After all, what is the use of trying out a lot of different horses if you have no idea what kind of load you are going to pull?

Some salespeople present product knowledge cafeteria-style, such as, "I will tell you everything I know about this pen and you tell me if there is anything about it that you like." This is a waste of time and is guaranteed to put the prospect to sleep!

How much better it is to qualify the customer first, determining what turns him on and then selecting from your own menu of product knowledge before you say a word. If you are acquainted with the customer, you should do this prior to the call. If not, you will need to do a bit of verbal probing at the beginning of the call, to see where the interests lie.

Transparency #5

Rapp's Law #4: Two sure-fire ways to kill the sale:
   A. Product knowledge that is interesting to you
   B. Technical jargon

Now for the fifth and final law of product knowledge.

Transparency #6

Rapp's Law #5: Don't Kick the Customer's Dog

This means, simply, don't criticize a product the customer is presently stocking or using. Think about how you feel when someone runs down an item that you own. It's not a very good way to put the prospect in a buying mood, is it? When you do this, you are really saying that the buyer made a mistake or used poor judgment in a previous purchase.

Instead, use a positive approach. Tell the customer about all of the additional benefits he or she will receive with your product, and you won't have to kick the customer's dog at all.

There are many benefits when you understand completely the competitive lines, not the least of which is that you are seen as an expert for the whole market. You are viewed as a writing instrument specialist or as a marker specialist. This is another aid to confidence building, mentioned earlier.

Let me quickly summarize our discussion. I started by saying that product knowledge by itself is sterile, if not useless. I used the example of product knowledge of a new automobile.

Then I said there are five laws of product knowledge you should remember.

Transparency #7

1. It's not having it that is important, it is knowing how to use it.
2. P.K. x G.S. = Cs and Cc.
3. Always put the cart before the horse.
4. Two sure-fire ways to kill the sale:
    a. Product knowledge that is interesting to you
    b. Technical jargon
5. Don't kick the customer's dog.

©Dartnell Corporation

A list of topics for workshops or seminars

Many sales meetings have an hour or so set aside for training. Trying to cover too many topics in such a short time is not usually effective. It's better to pick a single, narrow topic and concentrate on it. For example, spend the hour on opening statements and how to make them get the prospect's attention and interest, rather than trying to teach the entire sales presentation.

Here are some topics to consider:

1. Individual parts of sales presentations: opening statements, closings, etc.
2. Sales presentations on a specific product
3. Sales presentations to a specific type or size customer or prospect
4. Benefit statements (and features)
5. Strongest reason to buy
6. Best fear-of-loss statement
7. Proof statement
8. Listening
9. Probing questions
10. Demonstrating
11. Success stories
12. Using pauses, silence, restatements, and paraphrasing
13. Appeal to pride
14. Getting appointments
15. Cold calls
16. Written presentations
17. Profit projections, return-on-investment proposals
18. Body language
19. Routing
20. Time management
21. Developing trust
22. Setting goals

©Dartnell Corporation

Section 10

Humor in Sales Meetings

Okay, why did the chicken cross the road? If you have one or maybe two answers to that one, and fast, you have some idea of what humor is all about.

The obvious answer is, of course, to get to the other side. But there are as many answers as there are human beings in your audience, and that more or less is the definition of humor. A philosopher once described humor as absurdity confronting reality. That philosopher was Groucho Marx, who, more than being just a comedian, was a genuine wit.

How does this fit in with the idea of humor in sales meetings? Simply stated, a sales meeting without some levity is a month in the country. Those who don't see and appreciate the humor in their daily tasks and rounds are not likely to be the sort of salespeople you should have.

The problem with humor at sales meetings is to 1) keep it from getting scatological and 2) keep it from demanding the obligatory laugh. Humor, too, is a fragile flower; it lasts but a moment and should be savored at that moment.

Most good sales managers have a built-in sense of humor. It comes from knowing Martha, Joe, Karen, Mike, and Pete. It comes from riding herd on an obstreperous group, all of whom may respect you, but will break their behinds for you if they think you know how to laugh at yourself.

The purpose of humor at a sales meeting is, first of all, to lighten tension, which is not an easy task. Everyone is assembled and the boss *very much* in evidence, perhaps frowning. He's paying the bills! So what's your opener?

Rules for using humor

If you are not a stand-up comedian—and have the good sense to know it—the jokes in your repertoire should always reflect your own personality and style. There is nothing more painful, and even embarrassing, than a labored jest read from a script and devoid of nuance. Thus, the first rule is: Never read a joke.

Used properly and naturally, humor is an essential part of any sales meeting, if for no other reason than that it breaks the ice in what is frequently a formal setting. It also immediately establishes a link between the speaker and the audience. If it is a good joke and well told, the speaker is off and running, secure in the attention of his or her audience.

An opening joke is even better if the joke has a context link to whatever is under discussion. However, in searching for a context link, avoid the temptation to base the joke on someone in the room. Every organization has its house clown, someone who is the butt of his or her colleagues' humor. This sort of good-natured jesting is acceptable and even amusing in private, but out of place in a sales meeting setting.

The second rule, therefore, is: Don't pick on anyone in the group as the butt of any joke.

The third rule is: Never tell any off-color, ethnic, or racial jokes. It should go without saying—but too often does not—that ethnic, racial, and off-color jokes are strictly taboo. For one thing, they are not funny as a rule; for another, they are insulting to the audience and they demean the speaker.

The question arises next as to when to use humor and how much of it.

Some rules apply here as well. For example, use as much humor as possible at the start of the meeting. This serves to loosen things up and establish a teamwork approach to the work ahead.

Indeed, in preparation for the sales meeting it is a good idea to start collecting and sorting out jokes far in advance, trying out a few

©Dartnell Corporation

on family and friends. This way you can determine which jokes are superior or, more important, which jokes you tell well and which dovetail with your personality.

When you land on a favorite joke, commit it to memory and use it for your opening at the meeting. There are no guarantees on this, but you're on safer ground by having a pre-tested joke for your opening rather than one that you may have heard going into the meeting.

The fourth rule is: Open with your strongest joke.

Also, it is a good idea to suggest to each speaker that he or she use a touch of humor in his or her opening. The reason for this is the same as before: To establish camaraderie with the audience.

There are times, too, in any sales meeting when humor of any kind is inappropriate. Avoid jokes or veiled sarcasm during the serious parts of the meeting. For example, the talk by the company's comptroller, whether it imparts good news or bad, is no time for levity; nor is discussion of company policy changes a framework for joking. Laughter at this time is inappropriate because it lessens the impact of the serious material you are trying to get across. A human being is capable of only one concentrated emotion at a time. If that emotion is laughter, the serious side of the situation at hand is diminished.

The fifth rule is, then: Use humor only when appropriate, not during the serious sections of the meeting.

Next we get to the question of what is funny. Even such masters as Henny Youngman and Bob Hope admit they are not sure 100 percent of the time what is funny and, between the two of them, they have been breaking up audiences for well over 100 years.

Humor is hard to define—and even harder to perform!—because it is so very personal. The best rule of thumb to use in selecting a joke is to pick those you like best, those that gave you a chuckle or even a guffaw when first you heard them. Chances are, your taste will not be all that unusual.

A few guidelines on just what is funny might be helpful. What are known as context jokes work best as a rule at sales meetings. These jokes are basically anecdotes related to the business and involving a salesperson(s). Salesmen jokes—and we don't mean the off-color variety here—always are popular at sales meetings, and little wonder. Most of your audience relates immediately to the situation.

So, the sixth rule is: In selecting a joke or jokes, pick the ones that you find most amusing. Chances are, a lot of people will agree with you.

All of us know people who are great storytellers, who seem to come up with a new one every day and who are capable of breaking up a party just by opening their mouths. Unfortunately, most of us do not fall into that category. Some people can't remember a joke an hour after hearing it. Others spoil the joke by ruining the punch line or by dragging it out endlessly.

Those of us in the latter category would do well to keep a file of jokes going, not so much to break up the gang at the beach club, but to be ready when next we have to open a sales meeting or give a speech. This little file should be highly selective. But if you're like many of us, you get the joke down on paper fast before it is forgotten only to hear it used months later by someone else at a convention.

Some jokes, too, have a short shelf-life because of their topical nature. Ronald Reagan jokes aren't big anymore. Try to concentrate in your file on non-topical humor. These generally can be updated to conform to whatever rides the headlines this week.

While a personal joke file can prove invaluable, there are also standard reference works on humor, some of which are decidedly unfunny in their attempts to codify humor. The best reference work is probably the oldest and simplest, *Joe Miller's Jokebook*, which has been in print for decades but which contains the standard framework for many of the jokes we hear daily.

The seventh rule is: Keep a private (and small) file of your favorite jokes, updating it only when you hear what to you is a real thigh-slapper.

Standard jokes

The following, and variations thereon, are examples of old standards.

Humor in Sales Meetings

Closing
- A salesperson returned to the branch headquarters and reported, "I got two orders today from Henry Thresher." (This tough customer had never bought one penny's worth previously.)
  "From Henry Thresher?" someone exclaimed. "What were they?"
  "Get out and stay out."
- I will admit one thing: the salesperson who is afraid to close is colorful . . . *yellow!*

General
- "Not interested" doesn't cool off a good salesperson. He's heard it too often—from people who bought.
- The best time for a salesperson to say *nothing* is when a prospect wants to say something.
- The salesperson who knows his business gets the business.
- The big shot sales manager was approached by six little Girl Scouts selling cookies. "Why do you want to sell me?" he asked.
  "Because you are so handsome," smiled one of the girls.
  He bought 12 boxes and went back to his desk murmuring, "There are no better sales tools than truth and honesty."
- A dealer called the manufacturer and asked when he was going to get shipment on his last order. "When you pay your bill," was the answer.
  "Cancel the order," said the dealer. "I can't wait that long."
- The greatest salesperson I ever heard of was the one who sold a milking machine to a farmer with two cows and then took one cow as a down payment.

Getting the buyer's attention
Holding someone's complete attention for any length of time is impossible. Hugo Mussterberg of Harvard used to illustrate the point by telling of the alchemist who sold a recipe for turning eggs into gold. The buyer was to put the yolks of a dozen eggs into a pan and stir the yolks for a half hour without ever thinking of the word "*hippopotamus.*" Thousands tried, but none succeeded. If people can't keep their attention on one thing for 30 minutes for a pan of gold, they aren't likely to succeed for the privilege of listening to your sales talk. So get attention quickly, then press on to develop interest.

- "You lied to me," said the farmer to a salesperson. "I handled that mule like a baby, and yet I can't get him to do a single lick of work."

    "Let's go out and have a look at him," said the salesperson.

    They went to the farm. The mule was standing hitched to a plow. He wouldn't budge. The salesperson picked up a heavy stick and broke it over the mule's head. "Now try him," he said.

    "Giddap," said the farmer and the mule started off. "I don't understand this," the farmer said. "I'm sure that you told me I'd have to treat this mule gently."

    "You do," said the salesperson. "But first you have to get his attention."

Selling benefits

- A new hot dog barker at a baseball game came in to resign during the third inning. Asked why, he said, "Can't get through the crowd—people won't move when I ask them to." He was told to watch a veteran barker. He found the veteran saying, "Clear the way, please. Don't get mustard on your shirts."

Skill

- The priest and rabbi were playing golf. Before each putt the priest would say a short prayer. The rabbi, who was losing the game on the green, said, "Do you suppose if you taught me that prayer, I could sink those kinds of putts?"

    "Not a chance," answered the priest.

    "Why not?" demanded the rabbi.

    "Because you're a terrible putter," said the priest.

- You may be like the young fellow who came to his boss the second day on the job and asked for a lot more money because he was so inexperienced. He explained, "It's so much harder when you know so little."

Supervision

- One day a pathetic-looking little man walked into a booking agent's office and announced that he had developed a new act for vaudeville. He wanted to have the opportunity to show it to the booking agent. After a great deal of argument, the agent finally consented.

©Dartnell Corporation

The would-be actor began his curtain speech by explaining that his act starts in where the Wright brothers left off. He had discovered a way to fly without using any wings, motors, propellers or other mechanical contrivances. To prove this, he began to wave his arms frantically, and then suddenly his body rose into the air. At the same time he started to kick his feet.

Thus waving his arms and kicking his feet, he proceeded to flit around the room for about five minutes. Then he made a graceful landing back on his feet and said to the agent, "Well?"

The booking agent shrugged his shoulders and answered, "It's all right, I guess, but can you do anything besides imitate birds?"

In other words, don't be overly demanding.

Training

- A young salesman walked into my office one day and used the worst approach I have ever heard. He said, "You don't want to buy any life insurance, do you?"

  Well, he was right, I didn't; but this kid needed help. I said, "Young man, you'll never make a living like that! It's obvious you have no self-confidence, and confidence is what you need to sell insurance. Now I'm going to buy a policy, not because I need it, but to help build your confidence."

  While he was writing up the policy, I tried to give him a few pointers on sales techniques that would help him. As he was leaving, I tried to drive home one final point. I said, "Young man, what you should do is develop a list of several standard openings, memorize them, and use them."

  "I do," he said. "That was my opener for sales trainers."

- A father and son, from way back in the hills, were walking down a dirt road. A car drove by and the boy turned to his father and said, "What's that, Dad?"

  The father replied, "Shucks, son, I don't rightly know."

  A while later a train went by and the boy asked, "What's that, Dad?"

  The father replied, "Shucks, son, I don't rightly know."

An airplane flew overhead, and the boy again asked, "What's that, Dad?"

The father replied, "Shucks, son, I don't rightly know."

Son said, "Dad, do you mind me asking all of these questions?"

"Why, no, son, if you don't ask questions, you'll never learn anything!"

Driving a single point home is better than leaving three on base.

- A military recruit chose the infantry, instead of joining the paratroopers where the pay was much higher. When asked by a friend for the reason for his choice, he said, "I don't want to do nothing where the first time you do it, you gotta do it right."

- There was this fiddle player who was entertaining at a barn dance, and when he finished one particular song, some of the people asked for an encore. But one ornery character wasn't too impressed, and he yelled, "If ya got it right the first time, ya wouldn't a been called back t'do it agin."

Work habits

- Why is it? We never have enough time to do the job right, but we always have enough time to do it over.
- The trouble with these how-to-succeed books is that you find out from them that you have to work for it.
- A man's biggest mistake is to believe that he's working only for someone else.
- One of the greatest labor saving inventions of today is tomorrow.
- The salesperson who never does more than he gets paid for never gets paid for more than he does.
- "How long does it take you to get to work every day?"
  "Oh, about an hour after I arrive at the store."

**Attitude
(It's all in your point of view.)**

- The only difference between stumbling blocks and stepping stones is how you use them.

Change

- There are two kinds of fools. One says, "This is old, therefore it is good." The other says, "This is new, therefore it is better."

©Dartnell Corporation

Listening
- Professor asked Jones, "Why don't you enter into the discussion?" Jones said, "I learn more by listening. Anything I would say I already know."
- A wise old owl sat in an oak,
  the more he heard the less he spoke;
  the less he spoke the more he heard.
  Why can't we be like that wise old bird?
- A small boy was brought to a clinic for examination by his mother, an extremely talkative woman. During the preliminary quiz period, the doctor noticed that the boy didn't seem to be paying much attention to the questions. "Do you have trouble hearing?" he asked.
  "No," the boy replied, "I have trouble listening."

Talking
- When he talks he reminds me of a Texas steer. There's a point here, a point there, and an awful lot of bull in between.
- During a pause in a long, tiring speech, one guest said to another, "What follows this speaker?" Said the second guest, "Wednesday."
- The Bible tells us that Samson slew 10,000 Philistines with the jawbone of an ass. And we're losing sales every day for the same reason—talking too much.
- He's the kind of speaker who's here today and here tomorrow.

Writing
- "Why did you fire that secretary you had?"
  "She couldn't spell, she kept asking me how to spell every other word when she took dictation."
  "And you couldn't stand the interruptions?"
  "It wasn't that. I just didn't have time to look up all those words."

Definitions
- A conservative is a man who does not think that anything should be done for the first time.
- Conference: the only place where a group of important people who can do absolutely nothing by themselves can save face by doing nothing as a group.

©Dartnell Corporation

- Discussion: an argument where you just keep talking and talking and don't throw anything.
- A consultant: one who borrows your watch, tells you the time, and then charges you for it.
- Logic is an organized procedure for going wrong with confidence and certainty.
- Perfect product: costs a dime, sells for a dollar, and is habit forming.
- Good salesperson: one who sells goods that don't come back to customers who do.
- Super-salesperson: a man who can make his wife feel sorry for the girl who left her lipstick in his car.

Inspirational

- Success is a journey, not a destination.
- It's often the last key on the ring that opens the door.
- You can't help another person without helping yourself. When you row someone across the stream, you get there, too.
- Latent abilities are like clay—it can be mud on shoes, brick in a building, or a statue that inspires. The clay is the same. The result depends on how it is used.

Knowledge

- Those of you who think you know it all are particularly annoying to those of us who do.
- It isn't the things you don't know that get you into trouble; it's the things you know for sure that aren't so.

Learning

- Book salesperson to farmer: "Buy this book for $10, and you'll know twice as much about raising hogs as you do now."
    Farmer: "Shucks, I ain't raising hogs now half as good as I know how to."
- We can all profit by mistakes, particularly if our competition makes enough of them.
- Your mind is like a parachute. If you expect it to work, it first has to be open.
- "How come you can remember names so well?"
    "I took that Sam Carnegie course."

©Dartnell Corporation

- Three things a sales manager needs: One is a good memory, the other two I forget.
- I hear, and I forget. I see, and I remember. I do, and I understand.—Chinese proverb.

Management

- Executive ability is deciding quickly and getting somebody else to do the work.
- He's the kind of guy that would vote a town dry—and then move!
- A good executive not only knows how to take advice, but also how to reject it.
- No man will ever be a big executive who feels that he must, either openly or under cover, follow up every order he gives and see that it is done—nor will he ever develop capable employees.
- A good manager gets things done without quibbling.
- Somebody once asked a little boy, "Who destroyed the walls of Jericho?" The little boy said, "I didn't do it."

    His teacher said, "He's truthful, he probably didn't."

    The principal said, "The teacher's truthful. If she says he didn't do it, he didn't do it."

    The superintendent said, "Quit passing the buck. Send out for bids and let's get it fixed."

Motivation

- Wife, on golden wedding anniversary: "John, do you love me?"

    John: "Now Mary, I told you when I married you that I loved you, and if I ever change my mind, I'll let you know."
- It's about the golfer who landed in a sand trap. He is desperately trying to get out of the trap. He gets his nine-iron out and is swinging at the ball, but keeps missing it. Each time he swings, he hits the sand; the sand goes all over, and, with the sand, go many ants because the ball is sitting on top of an anthill.

    In desperation, one of the worker ants goes down the anthill hole to the queen's chamber and makes his report to the queen. He says, "We're in a desperate situation. Hundreds of workers are being killed by a very poor golfer, and we don't know what to do. He keeps hitting at the ball and keeps missing, and each time he hits the sand, hundreds of our workers are being killed. It is apparent he is never going to hit that ball."

"I'll go up myself and take a look," says the queen. So she follows the worker up the hole, and the sound of the swinging and the dying ants grows louder.

She climbs out, looks the situation over, and says, "Well, the conclusion is obvious. If you want to stay alive, you'd better get on the ball."

- During a survey of selling techniques, we asked a salesperson, "How long have you been working at this store, Mr. Walters?" "Ever since the manager threatened to fire me," he answered promptly.

Writing and use of Reports

- The Internal Revenue Service called the minister of a church and asked him a question about a $5,000 contribution that a member of the church showed on his income tax return as having been made to the church.

    "Can you tell me if he made such a contribution?"

    Replied the minister, "I don't know, I will have to check the records. But I will say this—if he hasn't, he will!"

- Salesperson being interviewed: "I left the last place for reasons of health. The boss threatened to kill me."

To close a meeting

- Abraham Lincoln was fond of telling the story of the man lost in the woods at night during a violent thunderstorm. Loud thunder rolled across the pitch black sky. Occasionally, a flash of lightning would light up the woods. After wandering aimlessly for a long time, the poor man dropped to his knees and raised his head to heaven in prayer. "Dear God, if it's all the same to you, I'd like a little less noise and a little more light." I hope this meeting has given you more light than noise.

- As Lady Godiva said when she neared the end of her famous ride, "I'm drawing toward my clothes."

Humor in Sales Meetings 107

Convention closing
- And so, as we head home with faith in our hearts, information in our minds, bills in our pockets, and towels in our luggage.
- "Just sittin' and wishin'
  Ain't gonna change your fate;
  The Lord provides the fishin',
  But you gotta dig the bait."

To open a meeting
- This sales manager had a salesperson who just wasn't cutting it. He never made quota. Nothing the manager did seemed to work. One day the company announced a training program.

  The sales manager decided to send this person, after all else had failed. When the salesperson returned, it didn't take long before sales soared.

  The sales manager couldn't understand it. He called in the salesperson and asked what happened. He said, "I don't know; things just seem to be going well."

  Sales manager: "Well, tell me what you do on a sales call."

  Salesperson: "Well, I just call on the prospect, like the other day I called on _____. He told me that his boy just graduated from Harvard with honors and I said, 'Fantastic,' and he gave me an order."

  Manager: "There must be more to it than that. Tell me more."

  Salesperson: "Well, I called on this other guy, and he told me how great a golfer he is. He said he just won the club tournament. I said, 'Fantastic,' and he gave me an order.

  "Another guy I called on told me he was a sailboat racing buff and had just won the local regatta. I said, 'Fantastic,' and he gave me an order."

  Manager: "Tell me, did you always say 'fantastic'?"

  Salesperson: "No, I used to say 'horse manure!!'"

- This sales meeting will now come to order, to see if we can get our customers to do likewise.
- While lecturing to a group at the end of a long, hard day one of the salespeople in the back started to doze. The instructor said, "You can't sleep in my class."

©Dartnell Corporation

The trainee said, "I could if you didn't talk so loud."

- As I understand it, my job is to talk to you. Your job is to listen. If you finish before I do, I hope you'll let me know.

Stunts

- Here is a good method to help the instructor and class learn the names of all participants quickly. It shows that you can remember names if you try. This will work with a class of up to 30 participants.

Procedure:

1. Have the first person stand and give his or her name.
2. The second person must give the first person's name and his or her own.
3. The third person must give the first two names, plus his or her own and so on until the last person names everyone in the room.

Rules:

1. Use first and last names (nicknames, if appropriate).
2. No notes are allowed, and name cards or tags are removed from sight prior to starting.
3. Help those who have trouble, but keep going.

- Use two dice, one with only 5s and the other with 6 and 2. Ask for a volunteer. Tell this person that you guarantee that these dice are not loaded, but that you will bet he or she will win with them. After two throws of 7 or 11, describe the dice. The point is this: You will win if you eliminate the chance of failure.

Section 11

Showmanship in Meetings

Balance, a sage once wrote, is the most desirable goal of the human condition.

The same might be said of balance as a goal when it comes to the use of showmanship in meetings. When too little showmanship is tucked into the serious material, you risk inattention and boredom; with too much showmanship, you risk overwhelming the serious aspects inherent in any business gathering.

When it comes to showmanship in a sales meeting, the organizer is cast in the unlikely role of a theatrical producer. He or she must hold the audience and give the people something to go home with other than smiles on their faces.

Again, the word is *balance*. There has been a tendency in recent years, particularly during the past five or so, for sales meetings to go the sobersides route: "We're here for business, not fun." This can be attributed to the mean-and-lean quest of top management, itself an outgrowth of the merger-takeover mania. Management never wants to appear frivolous in the eyes of stockholders. Gala sales meetings, complete with star comedians and ice shows at the final banquet, are much too costly and are out these days.

However, eliminating the more showy aspects of showmanship doesn't mean that a certain lightheartedness is not appropriate in these lean-and-mean days; in fact, quite the contrary. Showmanship is an essential ingredient in the sales meeting mix.

Why is showmanship so vital when running a sales meeting? Basically, it is important because you catch more flies with honey than with vinegar. Study after study in psychology labs at major

©Dartnell Corporation

universities has shown that memory retention increases markedly in most people when a fact is presented 1) in its context and 2) amusingly or dramatically. The latter is nothing more or less than showmanship. Take a lesson from the TV commercials.

If your sales meeting must be more than a social get-together of people who just happen to work for the same firm, it is essential that you send the sales reps back to their territories with a huge number of facts firmly implanted in their memories. Viewed in this light, showmanship is a necessary technique in a sales meeting to ensure memory retention.

Showmanship itself too frequently gets confused with one of its elements, humor. Showmanship includes humor, but is much more than that; it is the stage setting, the props, the lighting, the sound amplification, and whatever else goes into mounting a production, which in actuality is what a sales meeting amounts to.

We once knew a sales manager whose experience with little theater groups had made him expert in lighting. At that time, he worked for a large manufacturer of ready-made draperies, curtains, and bedspreads. The tradition in this industry is to hold two sales meetings a year, essentially for the purpose of introducing the new line to the sales force.

The meetings, coming as they did like clockwork every six months, tended to be dull. The line innovations and introductions were not all that breathtaking. The problem, then, was what to do to get some pizazz into the line presentation, the heart of this particular sales meeting?

Our friend wisely opted to make use of his stage lighting skills to inject some showmanship into the line presentation. It worked beautifully. Fabrics and designs that look boring when laid on a table and described as a new cotton-polyester blend suddenly came to life when back-lighted. Fabric designs highlighted by a pin spot in a darkened room took on their own identity. Instead of droning on under house lights about this or that fabric and its virtues, the sales manager had put on a show and created a note of glamor, which the fabrics otherwise lacked.

©Dartnell Corporation

The sales force was *impressed*, one of the main purposes showmanship at sales meetings can and should accomplish. Better still, this bit of showmanship fired up the sales force to imitate the boss on their customers' display floors, in turn creating a healthy increase in consumer interest and in sales.

Another reason to use showmanship at a sales meeting is to make some point or product *memorable*. In the example above, few members of the sales force were likely to forget a couple of the patterns so artfully lighted at the line presentation.

The same showmanship technique can, of course, take many forms, but the key is to accentuate the positive. This can be accomplished by humor, stunts, or any other unusual (but in context) technique of showmanship.

Last, but certainly not least, showmanship is important as a technique because, done properly, it *entertains*. By definition, showmanship implies something out of the ordinary, a departure from the routine. It can individualize a product or premise in anyone's mind. Knowing that you have a product that is *unique* is bound to make any salesperson happy.

There's never been a sales meeting, either, where things didn't lag on occasion; people are getting tired and everyone's in a slump under the barrage of information, vital as it is. When this happens, go into a showmanship mode for a minute or two. Wake them up; jar them to full attention. Sometimes this can have nothing at all to do with the content of the meeting, but can instead be a joke or a turn of phrase totally off-the-wall.

Once you've broken the tension, proceed on course, keeping an eye open for another lapse into ennui, which is bound to come. Thus, be prepared at times during the sales meeting to just plain entertain. This doesn't mean you have to be a stand-up comic, but it does mean you must be prepared to go into your act. Nothing is more painful than a stunt that misfires. This means that you should have a number of stunts in mind *before* the sales meeting and that you should have them well-rehearsed and down pat. Keep working at the stunts you intend to use until there is no margin of error on the big day. The same goes for jokes; rehearse these with your spouse or a patient friend until you have the timing correct. Most jokes depend on timing to work. Facial reactions from a spouse or friend while you are telling a gag can give you important clues on timing. Don't think for a minute, either, that Bob Hope just stands up there and tells jokes. No way. His are carefully written and arduously rehearsed before going out across the airwaves.

Whatever else it is, a sales meeting should never become a vaudeville show, meaning, again, that the key in the use of showmanship is *balance.*

Basically, you're not out to entertain, but to teach. You can do both at the same time. Think back to some of your favorite teachers in high school or college and you'll get the point of how teaching can go hand in hand with entertainment.

The late Edward Wagenknecht of the University of Washington was a master at combining teaching with showmanship. Those who were fortunate enough to have taken his English course in Shakespeare's sonnets will never forget either the sonnets or Wagenknecht, mainly because the good professor, in his zeal to impart the beauty of the material, acted out the sonnets; he didn't just read them and then give quizzes. It was a startling experience, to be sure, but it was effective.

Showmanship, however, can be totally out of place when overused or used at the wrong time. Don't allow the ham in you to take over completely, and avoid special forms of humor perhaps appreciated only by you and a few others. Also avoid overly subtle stunts, ones that you favor more for their shock value than for emphasizing a point you wish to impress on the minds of the sales force.

A good rule of thumb is to avoid attempts at humor or showmanship during any discussion of strictly financial or business reporting matters. Granted, these frequently can be humorous in themselves, but let the salespeople figure that out. They will anyway.

The sole exception to avoiding the use of showmanship during meeting segments dealing with business nuts and bolts might be during a discussion of proper filling in of sales reports and why they are necessary.

As all people in sales know, sales reports are the bane of most salespeople's lives. Your best people, very likely, are the worst at filling in sales reports adequately. This probably is because your best people knock themselves out during the day and are little inclined to sit at a desk in the evening and do the follow-up paperwork involved, except the writing up of orders.

Showmanship can also be a distraction during question and answer periods. There is too much of a temptation at this time to turn humor into criticism of an individual. Humor and sarcasm are not the same thing, although both can produce group laughter.

Another good rule of thumb is never to use showmanship when your individual taste tells you it is inappropriate. Many such occasions will arise during any sales meeting. A seasoned sales manager can see them coming.

Advantages

The advantages of showmanship can be summed up as follows:
1. To relieve tension.
2. To nail down key points.
3. To promote a feeling of group participation via laughter.
4. To highlight product features by special emphasis.
5. To impart pace and rhythm to the overall sales meeting.
6. To ensure that the sales meeting is an enjoyable experience, not an unrelieved drag.

Disadvantages

The disadvantages of showmanship, used incorrectly, are as follows:
1. The lurking danger of showing off.
2. The danger of overshadowing the content with the style.
3. The generation-gap difficulties in selecting the right music, pertinent stunts, gags, etc.
4. The temptation to overuse showmanship, thus obscuring the kernel message of the meeting.
5. Your own possible failings as a sort of toastmaster or master of ceremonies. Those with few skills in this area do best to

©Dartnell Corporation

rely on visual showmanship techniques and forget the patter.

6. The danger that humor can become too personal when a group of people know one another well. Watch out for sarcasm!

Again, we get back to balance. Used appropriately, showmanship has the effect of lightening up any sales meeting and, more importantly, of imparting a sense of professionalism to the proceedings. A sales meeting is, after all, a production of sorts.

However, by far the most important effect of showmanship on any meeting is the sense of well-being it engenders among people. It's the secret ingredient in producing a continuing upbeat mood at any meeting, no matter how serious the matters under discussion.

Ideas for showmanship

Here are fifteen tested ideas that work in using showmanship at a sales meeting:

1. Have the meeting room dimly lit as the audience files in to take seats, with the platform as dark as possible. When everyone is seated, beam a pin spot on the new product you will be focusing on during the meeting. Turn all lights out, and then bring house lights up. This works particularly well when the product in question is dramatic in itself, something the salespeople are not accustomed to seeing daily.

2. Announce at the start of the meeting that it is essential that the meeting stay on schedule and that to make sure it does you have arranged for musical interludes to start when time is running out on any segment. You can keep your own clock on the podium and signal your sound person when to turn on the music. This is an effective method of sticking to schedule and, because it is so inflexible, no one gets upset for being cut off in mid-sentence. Also, everyone present is familiar with the technique, since virtually all TV talk shows use it. The technique also will stir up the audience for the next segment, providing you use the right music. It's best to use fairly rhythmic music with an insistent beat. To

demonstrate what you have in mind, and without announcing what you are intending to do, cut yourself off in your introductory remarks with your own music cue. The salespeople will get the point fast.

3. To assist the audience in staying alert throughout an important (and perhaps dull) segment, announce that every time a certain word is used by a speaker, the first person to yell out "key" will get a prize. But be sure the key word is a common enough one so that you'll be sure to use it. If for some reason you find you haven't used the word, make sure you do so casually in your presentation.

4. Pre-record on tape certain key points you wish to emphasize during your presentation. Then say, "Now here's what we've got to remember," and flip on the recorder. Your disembodied voice coming across on tape will have a jarring effect and assist in helping the salespeople remember crucial information.

5. Use a meeting theme to give continuity of expression to the entire meeting. This theme can be anything appropriate to your particular gathering, but it should be emphasized during each segment and the theme should be prominently emblazoned over the speaker's platform.

6. Use a trumpet fanfare for each new product when making a line presentation. The fanfare also is a good idea when you are holding an awards presentations or when making a major personnel announcement or introduction.

7. Plant a heckler in the audience. Have the heckler bring up either common complaints that you think may be on the minds of your people or frequent customer objections. Answer each one as it comes up, or ask your salespeople to answer it.

8. Use magic. Pull a new product out of the hat or make things appear and disappear. Since it's not likely that you or your staff can do this, hire a local magician. Their fees are amazingly low. A short meeting with the magician will most likely produce a dozen ideas appropriate to your meeting.

9. Have a marching band, drum and bugle corps, or a singing group enter the back of the meeting room to help announce a new product, service, or promotion.

10. Wear a costume and talk about your product as it would have been discussed by a historical figure (Julius Caesar, Shakespeare, George Washington).

11. Try a skit. Select several of your people who like to act and are real hams. Get together and create a simple story. For example, you may want the group to act out the wrong way to sell a product, followed by the right way.

    Another idea would be to have two actors play the roles of buyer and seller. Instruct the actors that they can say only what a person in the audience tells them to say. Set up a specific selling situation. Let's say it's a cold call and the salesperson will be asking qualifying questions. Start by asking the audience to decide what the first question will be. The salesperson on stage then asks the question and the customer responds. You again ask the audience to choose the next question, etc. This can be very funny and very enlightening at the same time. You can think of many variations of this situation, I'm sure.

    When planning skits, be sure to keep them short and simple. If there's time, do a rehearsal prior to the meeting. Always explain to the audience why you're doing the skit; immediately following the skit, review what was learned.

12. To build a team effort, you may want to give everyone a T-shirt with a new product or slogan on it. Hats and caps are also popular. Be dramatic when you distribute these items for maximum effectiveness.

13. Place a large "mystery box" on stage, with no indication as to its contents. At the appropriate time, open the box and reveal the mystery. It could be a new product, a premium or incentive, or it could be filled with money, which represents bonuses your salespeople will receive if they successfully sell the new product or service.

14. Tape something to the bottom of each chair in the meeting room. At the appropriate time, ask everyone to look at the bottom of his or her chair. There are many variations to this gimmick. If the item was a dollar bill, you could say, "We put the money there to make the point that a successful salesperson must get up off his seat these days in order to make a buck." Instead of dollars, try using answers about a product. Ask each recipient to read his or her answer and to try to figure out the matching question. For example, one piece of paper might say, "reinforced plastic panel"; the question you're looking for is, "What material is used in the base of our new electronic scanner?"

15. Use props to make a point. This will be interesting and help your audience remember key points. Here are just a few. Use your imagination to come up with more.
    - Towel: crying towel, mop up the competition, etc.
    - Play money: illustrate profits, rewards
    - Hats: put on the customer's hat for a moment; same with shoes
    - Gloves: handle hot prospects; handle a certain customer with kid gloves
    - Map: to point out where we're headed
    - Mop: to mop up the competition
    - Large magnifying glass: hunt for prospects, get down to fine points
    - Ladder: steps to a sale; climb to higher and higher sales, etc.
    - Horn: to toot in celebration of a successful product launch
    - Shovel: planting the seeds for success
    - Drum: drumming up new business
    - Large clock: the importance of time
    - Baseball bat: improve your batting average
    - Football: gain yardage on the competition
    - Ten-foot pole: our competition can't touch us with a . . .

Section 12

Using Meeting Planners

There comes a time in every meeting planner's life when the question is, "How did I ever get myself involved in all of this?" The question usually arises for even the most seasoned planner at about the time your latest meeting is about to convene.

There you are awash in the details of an adventure that has no assurance of success, but plenty of chances for failure. As the song goes, "It all depends on you." Take heart! If you've done your detail work and learned to delegate some of the responsibilities, your fears are probably just a case of nerves.

The major problem among most meeting planners is that the world and routine go right along in tandem with all the work involved in planning and setting up a meeting. This includes, very likely, your full-time responsibilities elsewhere. The business doesn't grind to a halt semi-annually just because you have to stage a meeting. Then, too, as all meeting planners come to know, the best meetings are the ones that appear to be effortless and that run without a glitch. Getting a meeting to that stage translates into work, and lots of it.

Even relatively modest meetings, if run correctly, require enormous attention to detail and advance planning. They don't just burst, full-blown, from someone's enthusiasm the day before the meeting opens.

A realization on the part of top management in some of the largest corporations that meeting planning is a full-time job has brought on just such a job within the corporation. Sometimes this person runs an entire department devoted to planning and staging

©Dartnell Corporation

various meetings, with the boss of the department reporting to the overall director of sales.

Some major firms, also aware of the logistical problems involved in staging sales meetings, farm out this responsibility to their advertising or promotion agencies—for a healthy fee, of course. However, there still has to be an executive of the firm in overall charge, if for no other reason than to watch budgets and make sure that the meeting doesn't fly off into irrelevancy!

The most afflicted of meeting planners are those who work for medium or smaller-sized companies and who wear several hats within the firm, of which meeting planning is not the most important. These are the people who really need some help, even above and beyond the hopefully dedicated assistant or secretary.

Seeking outside help

While you might have trouble selling the idea within the boardroom, sometimes it is cost effective to seek outside help in planning and staging your sales meetings. For example, if the planning takes you away from the sales firing line too long, you are not really doing your primary job and sales very likely will suffer. It's simply a question of not being able to be in more than one place at once. As noted, this is a difficult concept to sell to top management, probably because of the days when sales conventions were widely viewed as social events with a little company hoopla thrown in to justify the cost. Now that sales meetings have become a primary management tool, the planning required has increased enormously.

The best way to convince management that sales meetings are more than social events is, of course, to emerge from a sales meeting with objectives flying. Again, that's something that doesn't happen without planning and plenty of hard work.

If you can wrangle budget approval for outside help in staging your meetings, you'll need to do some research into where best to seek that help. A good place to start is to contact friends in other industries who might currently employ meeting planners or consultants. If you enter this fray cold turkey, contact one of the organizations listed on page 124 for advice or help, but most particularly for leads.

Be advised that most firms or individuals you would wish to hire for planning and staging services are expensive, with billing usually done on an hourly rate, much like billing from an ad agency.

Working with the outside planner

If you luck out with your meeting planner and get one who knows sales problems, knows how to listen, and is good at detail and billing procedures, you'll be not only pleased but relieved of a lot of work. If you don't luck out, you probably will bring on a lot more work than if you'd run the show yourself from scratch. That's why it is important right from the start to establish a good (and frank) working relationship with any outside planner. Is he or she realistic? Is he or she low-key and efficient? Does the planner have some knowledge of sales problems, techniques, and—most important—salespeople? Also, is the planner a quick study? In other words, does he or she grasp the dynamics of your firm without a lot of hand-holding?

Set a budget with the planner right from the start and make it crystal clear that this budget has no fat in it. Then ask what the planner can offer for the fee. This negotiation should take place right at the beginning of your interview. It is important to impress on the person that 1) there will be no budget overruns and 2) you expect all services promised in the written proposal to be carried out as scheduled.

If you are fortunate enough to establish a good rapport with your potential planner, chances are that he or she will get a quick and sure grasp of what kind of meeting you wish and what problems you wish to have addressed, as well as what back-up equipment will be needed. Sometimes planners handle only certain sections of the meeting, such as the booking of space, meals, transportation, and presentations. Others run the entire show, from notifying salespeople to tipping the banquet waiters and booking the speaker(s). How much they do depends, of course, on the fee and also on the drive and energy of the planner you retain.

The major danger in retaining a planner is the possibility that your meeting may descend into superficiality—all show and little substance. Stress from the start that the meeting basically is to be an educational project.

Putting a company employee in charge

As an alternative to going through the rigors of training and working with an outside planner, you might wish to designate someone within your organization as being in charge of the meeting, preferably someone who has worked closely with you on past meetings, knows what you want, and knows which buttons to push internally to make things happen.

This alternative, in fact, generally proves most satisfactory, if you just don't pass on a burden to someone already struggling with other responsibilities. In other words, figure out how much time you spend on planning and staging meetings and make sure the person you appoint internally has the time to do the job properly. Certainly this, too, is an added expense, but the great advantage of having an in-house planner is that you see this person every day and can thrash out problems face to face without long lunches or having to spell everything out in writing. Look around your own department. Very likely the assistant who has been so much help in meetings past is more than eager to take over the job.

Combining alternatives

You might also consider delegating a great deal of the nuts-and-bolts meeting planning to that loyal assistant, while utilizing to the fullest the service of a hotel staff for lodging, food, and set-up needs. If you have worked with a particular hotel or convention manager before and have come to respect the way he or she gets things done, why not rely on this person for more of the detail planning? Generally these people are highly skilled in handling the logistics of meetings, large or small. The only thing they don't get involved with is the content of the meeting, which is where an assistant under your guidance comes in.

Using a consultant

Instead of going whole hog and farming out the entire meeting to a planner, you may wish to go the route of retaining the services of a consultant, who comes a bit cheaper than a planner. However, if the

©Dartnell Corporation

consultant is not experienced, you will merely end up with someone else to supervise. Because of the great growth in the number and size of meetings and conventions in recent years, there are firms specifically staffed and run to consult on the logistics and planning of sales meetings. The list of names presented at the end of this section for help in finding planners also can be used to find consultants. You might also wish to check your local phone directory under *management consultants* for assistance. Some such firms do not get involved in consulting on in-house matters such as sales meetings, but others do. Those who don't may be able to recommend those who do.

The media specialist

Dealing with the media is another area in which you may profitably use outside help, thereby saving yourself a lot of aggravation. Media specialists are those who are expert at audio-visual presentations, booking entertainment packages, and staging shows. If your meeting is a large and complex one in terms of programs and the need for audio-visual aids, hiring outside media specialists can save you countless hours and, usually, a lot of money.

Before contacting such specialists it is important that you break out and budget those elements of your program requiring the firm's services. It is almost as simple as saying to them, "Here's what I have to spend and here's what I want to accomplish." Then let them come to you with a proposal. Since these firms, usually well known to the management of large hotels, are in daily contact with suppliers, stage personnel, and entertainers, you are relieved of the chore of tracking down a lot of people and hiring them individually. These media firms also know local market conditions and know who and what will be available for the dates you have booked.

The following associations can be of help in providing leads to meeting planners and consultants:

Meeting Planners International
INFOMART
1950 Stemmons Freeway
Dallas, TX 75207
(214) 746-5222

Society of Corporate Professionals
2600 Garden Road, Suite 208
Monterey, CA 93940

Sales & Marketing Executives International
Statler Office Tower, Suite 446
Cleveland, OH 44115

Hotel Sales & Marketing Association International
1300 L Street NW, Suite 800
Washington, DC 20005

Exhibit Designers & Producers Association
1411 K Street NW
Washington, DC 20005

American Hotel & Motel Association
1201 New York Avenue, NW, Suite 600
Washington, DC 20005

©Dartnell Corporation

Section 13

Speakers and Workshop Leaders

If you're adding sales training to your meetings, you may want to utilize one of your own training people, such as the sales training manager or another person in your company holding that responsibility. There are a number of benefits to using someone other than yourself or your own staff to conduct training. First of all, these other individuals may have considerable experience and credibility in the areas you want them to discuss, in which case they may be billed as subject matter experts.

Secondly, they may have many skills (such as being a workshop leader, instructor, or teacher) that are not available in your own sales organization. Whenever possible, we urge that you use your own corporate people if they are available and qualified.

Whenever possible, you should use training materials that fit the projects that you are working on at the time and particularly those projects that are being discussed at the sales meeting. While it would certainly be okay to do a workshop on cold calling at any time, if this is not your major objective for the next sales period or so, you might be better off to focus on what could help the salespeople immediately upon leaving the meeting.

As with any training program, you first must identify your specific needs—the training needs of the salespeople. This must be done before deciding on the subject for which the training will be developed and, more particularly, on how it will be delivered. Figures 1 and 2 on pages 126 and 127 show some forms and procedures to use in determining the training need at hand.

©Dartnell Corporation

Figure 1. Training Needs: What Are the Priorities?

Show Priority	Knowledge
_____	Knowledge of products or services. Which ones?
_____	Knowledge of the industry (industries)
_____	Knowledge of the marketplace
_____	Knowledge of geographic areas
_____	Knowledge of customers
_____	Knowledge of company/division goals and plans
_____	Technical knowledge (how used, etc.)
_____	Knowledge of prices, terms, delivery, etc.
_____	Knowledge of the expected future
_____	
_____	
_____	

Show Priority	Skills
_____	Basic selling skills
_____	Demonstration
_____	Call planning
_____	Time management
_____	Benefit selling
_____	Steps in the sales presentation
_____	Making appointments
_____	Cold calling
_____	Telemarketing
_____	Negotiating
_____	
_____	
_____	

©Dartnell Corporation

Figure 2. Meeting Outline for Speakers

Dear_____

   Thank you for accepting our invitation to address our forthcoming sales meeting. For your information, here are some important details about the meeting:

Firm name_____ Type of meeting_____

Location of meeting_____ Address_____

Date_____ Time meeting starts_____ Time it ends_____

Formal_____ Informal_____ Breakfast_____ Lunch_____ Dinner_____

Dress required: Business ( ) Black tie ( )

Speaker will be introduced by_____

Time of speech_____ Time allotted_____

Number of speakers_____ Speaker's place on program_____

Topic(s) we would like covered_____
_____
_____

Estimated attendance_____ Type of audience_____

Time speaker can leave meeting_____

Other events speaker is expected to attend:

Reception_____ Location_____

   Time_____

Meeting press_____ Location_____ Time_____

Directors' meeting_____ Location_____ Time_____

Arrangements

You will be met by_____ Firm_____

On arrival contact_____ Phone_____

Hotel accommodations at_____

Suggestions, remarks_____
_____
_____

   Please send us a biographical sketch, glossy photo, and title of your talk as soon as possible.

Sincerely,

_____   _____
         (Name)   (Firm)

©Dartnell Corporation

Determining training needs

As noted above, you really need to know what the training needs of your sales force are before putting a program together for your next sales meeting.

Keep in mind that group training is always a compromise, because not everyone needs the same training, or at least not to the same degree. Sometimes you have to aim for the middle, realizing that not everyone at your meeting will gain equally from the training. That's all the more reason to do as much tailoring as possible when you actually conduct the training. For example, you may want the brand new salespeople to work as a group, since their needs will be more basic.

A good place to start in determining training needs is to review the performance appraisals or reviews of each of your salespeople, to look for common needs. Your first-line sales supervisors or district managers should have a good idea of the needs of their people. If you employ a sales trainer, talk with him or her about possible needs. However, be aware that not all the shortcomings of your sales force can be fixed through training. If your people know how to complete their daily reports, but are not doing it, all the training in the world will be useless.

Here are a few questions to ask yourself and your people. The answers can lead you in a productive search of needs that, once fulfilled, will have a high payoff.

1. During the next 6 to 12 months, what will change in our company and in our marketplace that will require new knowledge and skills by our salespeople?
2. How can these new requirements best be met and what part(s) of them can best be handled at sales meetings?
3. What products or services will require extraordinary attention during the next few months and what kind of training will help in this effort?
4. Of all the training I could give, what would appeal most to my salespeople?
5. Of all the training I could give, what would appear to have the greatest return on investment? The second greatest return?

©Dartnell Corporation

6. What new products or services will we be introducing in the near future and what training will be needed by our sales force?
7. How can training help with the upcoming promotional efforts of our company?
8. Is this a good time to follow up on training provided earlier?
9. What kinds of educational efforts of past sales meetings were well accepted and appeared to produce the desired behavior changes?
10. For each type of training I'm considering, which can be most effectively given at a sales meeting?

Choosing a trainer

Now that you have identified the needs and given thought to how these needs might best be met, you can decide how the training can be best delivered and how much time will be necessary to do the job. Any experienced trainer will be able to delineate some of the training approaches in order to solve the problem. For example, he or she may decide that, for a particular basic selling skill, a lot of role playing practice will be most helpful. In another case, where new product knowledge must be learned, the trainer may decide that an audio-visual presentation, discussion, and testing will be the best approaches for your salespeople to learn about the new products. In another case, product demonstrations might be helpful.

If not already established, this is the point in time to decide who you will use to deliver the training. This may seem a bit late in the process. However, until you know what your needs are and how they can best be met, you wouldn't know if you need that instructor, that audio-visual expert or whether you can handle the entire program yourself.

If you decide that you need an audio-visual presentation or a video production, you should find those organizations and firms which specialize in this area, if such expertise does not exist within your own company. If you've not used a production company, you may want to talk to several, either in the area where your offices are located or, if it's going to be a stage production and/or a multi-media production, you may want to talk to people who are located in the city where your meeting will be held.

If you want to engage a workshop or seminar leader, and there is no one in your own company who can handle the work, you will need to look outside at trainers, consultants, or others who have experience in this area. Beware of the trainers or consultants who want to install their own programs into your schedule without first making any attempt to match them to your needs. Remember that it is always easier for the outside person to teach a program that they have developed and with which they are familiar. If they are not willing to tailor a program to your needs or to start from scratch with you, I would look for other trainers. Any training people worth their salt will want to do the best possible job for you and will want to help you solve your training problems. This can usually be done best by developing a special program for your needs. Although this costs more money, it may be worth it in the long run. If your budget does not allow for this, perhaps a tailoring of similar material will be possible.

Where do you find these outside people? The best place to start is by talking with people in your own organization who may have used similar trainers, talking with other sales managers who have used individuals in the past, and perhaps talking with associations such as The National Society of Sales Training Executives, American Management Association, American Society for Training and Development, and other non-profit groups.

Once you obtain names of several individuals, you should call them on the phone, discuss your situation, determine what their recommendations are, and what they feel the next step should be. Most, unless they're very busy, will be interested in helping you, but what you must determine is whether or not they are the right trainers for the people who need to be trained. This is difficult. You may want them to submit proposals or at least outlines of what they think will work best for you and, if they are nearby, perhaps visit with them person-to-person. In fairness to them, you will need to give them quite a bit of information before they can come up with anything that will come close to fitting your needs.

©Dartnell Corporation

Some sales managers and others who run meetings ask for proposals, but provide very little information in terms of the true situation that exists in their sales forces. You must be truthful with prospective trainers if you expect them to be helpful. If you have a serious problem with a sales force in a certain area or with particular salespeople, you must share this with the person who is developing the training for you.

After looking at several proposals and talking to several consultants or trainers, you should then select one who you think will do the best job for you. At this point in time, you should negotiate a fee with him or her and lock in the dates for the particular sales meeting. Be sure you have some sort of written contract and that the fee and expenses are specified. Now your work is only beginning, because you need to sit down with the trainer—spending as much time as is necessary—to develop the workshop or training program.

Developing the training program

Be sure that you see the entire program and review it with the consultant or trainer far in advance of the meeting. There should be no surprises. If you don't like what's being developed, it is your responsibility to make changes early so that the individual you have hired will have time to do the work. If you have others in your organization who are knowledgeable about training programs, you should check out the proposals and all the work being done by the outside person with your inside person several times during the development stages.

Finally, you should have a run-through or mock-up training program with the outside person prior to the start of the meeting. Anything that is to be presented, either verbally or audio-visually, should be run through with the trainer, making any last minute changes that you feel are necessary. Remember, it is not only what is being taught, and how it is being taught, but also the manner in which it is being presented; the speaking voice and the attitude of the trainer or trainers will have a significant impact on your trainees.

©Dartnell Corporation

All of this will come out in a practice session prior to the meeting. Even though this takes valuable time, it still should be done. Remember, once the program starts and the seminar workshop begins, there is almost nothing you can do to change it. The die has been cast.

Speakers and workshop leaders

One of the traditional components of any sales meeting has been the speaker, a word that has also evoked more groans than perhaps any other facet of a sales meeting program.

The negatives of overreliance on speakers should be apparent to any sales meeting veteran. Alas, such is not the case. There is hope, however, that this may change, because the younger generation of salespeople is no longer interested in the psycho-babble of many so-called and usually self-appointed experts, many of whom have written a quasi-psychological book on some phase of merchandising, which they have promoted vigorously on TV talk shows.

This sounds as if we're laying a blanket rap on speakers per se at sales meetings. While this is not so, what we are saying is this: choose your speaker with care.

When you feel it appropriate to insert a speaker segment into your sales meeting agenda, keep in mind that speakers come in two general categories: 1) the in-house expert, known to most of your salespeople, and 2) the outside expert in any given field.

If possible, always attempt to utilize the talents of your in-house experts in scheduling speeches at a sales meeting. The credibility quotient, for one thing, is far higher with in-house speakers—they know the firm, its problems, and the product.

Unfortunately, too often the reliable in-house expert, while talented and skilled in his or her field, may be a lousy public speaker. Some people just can't stand in front of a group and speak effectively. They may be great on a one-to-one basis, but when it comes to getting up in front of a group they either freeze, speak inaudibly, or give the impression of being a dunce. Thus, you frequently are left with no option but to seek an outside speaker who is competent on the topics you wish to stress.

©Dartnell Corporation

Anyone with experience in booking freelance speakers for sales meetings will tell you this is far easier said than done. Outside speakers, like in-house experts, can be categorized into two general classifications: the specialist and the entertainer. Go for the specialist in most cases and avoid the mini-celebrity who has built up a minor reputation as an expert on TV. The speaker with the least celebrity, real or assumed, very likely will be the most flexible in meeting your needs and better able to target his or her remarks to your agenda.

Before you finalize your meeting arrangements, be sure to check out your speaker. Check with other firms that have used the speaker. Remember that there are two primary considerations in choosing a speaker: 1) quality and content of the material covered by the speaker and 2) his or her effectiveness before an audience.

Sources

Here are a few good sources to use in recruiting speakers.

1. Employees of your own company, including officers and directors.
2. Movers and shakers within your particular industry.
3. Trade associations in which your firm holds memberships, such as the U.S. Chamber of Commerce, National Association of Direct Selling Companies, etc.
4. Watch the business sections of major newspapers and magazines and of your own trade press to build a list of potential speakers.
5. Encourage your own staff and key executives within your firm to report on outstanding speakers they have heard at meetings. To make sure you get reports of this nature, provide your staff and key executives with a little form to mail to you when he or she encounters a likely candidate for your own sales meetings.
6. Exchange speaker information with ten or so sales managers of your acquaintance. Have your exchange list represent as wide a variety of industries as possible. If one name keeps popping up as a pro, you can be sure your potential speaker possesses one quality you need: flexibility.

7. Offer to swap speakers from your own company with speakers from other firms.

In other words, the safest and most reliable method of securing skilled outside speakers is to network with other people of your acquaintance who also are charged with organizing sales meetings for their firms.

It's also a good idea to keep an updated file of possible speakers, rated by you and noting who recommended each. This file can be a big help when you are in the planning stages for your next meeting.

Dealing with outside speakers

There's a certain amount of protocol that goes into dealing with an outside speaker. Although most of this amounts to common courtesy, here are a few tips in this regard.

1. Start with a clear understanding of his or her fee and give the speaker an honest estimate on the number of people who will attend. Find out what props may be needed and make sure they are on hand. Send the speaker complete details of what is expected of him or her just as soon as you have concluded negotiations about fees and expenses.
2. If the speaker is coming from out of town, meet him or her at the airport; see that he or she is settled into a room and made comfortable. Then show the speaker the facilities and make sure all props are on hand.
3. Escort the speaker to the meeting place and introduce him or her around and make the person feel welcome. This is a good time to re-emphasize the amount of time allowed for the talk.
4. Keep your introduction short and make it as pointed as possible, avoiding a flowery introduction. Make sure the podium is well lighted and that the microphone is in working order.
5. Your duties as host don't end with the talk. Have the speaker escorted to the airport or, if staying overnight, see to it that the person is entertained properly.
6. When the speaker returns home, write him or her a sincere note of thanks and include all the publicity clips you have collected concerning his or her appearance at your sales meeting.

Courtesies of this nature are invaluable to your firm and will make your life a lot easier when next you need a speaker. In fact, professional speakers are much like any other group in that they know what's going on within their business. Your last speaker may be the best person to contact for names for the next speaker.

The form in Figure 2, page 127, can save you pages of typescript in adequately briefing your speaker in advance of the meeting.

Another important thing to remember when selecting a speaker for your meetings is always to tailor the speaker to the program, not the program to the speaker. Make it clear to the speaker, too, that you do not wish him or her to read from a prepared text. Even the most skilled public speakers sometimes can't avoid the drone syndrome when reading a speech, no matter how pertinent and valuable its content. Eye contact is all important in an effective speech and this is all but impossible when the speaker must continually refer to text. Most professional speakers, of course, do work from prepared texts, but they rarely let the audience in on that fact.

Determining fees

The question now arises: How much can you afford to invest in this speaker?

If you luck out, and avoid the temptation to book a mini-celebrity merely for his or her name value, the cost of a good speaker probably will not be as high as you might imagine.

Don't be scared off by what you read in the consumer press about the fees some celebrity speakers command. It's not likely you will want to book a retired general, a famous newspaper columnist, or a celebrated author of how-to books. You're more likely to want a more narrowly focused expert, and they are available in virtually all fields.

Most professional speakers employ agencies to handle their bookings and fees, saving you negotiating face-to-face with the speaker. Most fees are negotiable. Only the so-called stars of the public speaking circuit can afford to stick to precisely the fee his or her agent might first propose. Much depends on how busy the speaker is, how close the engagement is to his or her home, and even how interested the speaker is in the proposed topic. Therefore, don't immediately accept the proposed fee. Chances are, that's the outside price.

The best way to handle a fee negotiation is to be perfectly frank. Say, for example, "Well, I can't afford that. All my budget will permit is (name figure). Can you suggest anyone else?"

Upon hearing this, the agent, or perhaps even the speaker, may very well agree to some price concessions or compromises, but don't press your luck. Keep the negotiation on a friendly and impersonal level.

The best method to use in keeping down speakers' costs is, of course, to rely on in-house experts, on whom you doubtless can prevail to participate without additional cost to your firm. Be sure to determine in advance that your in-house expert is capable of standing in front of an audience and making sense. Most professional speakers earn every dime they make.

©Dartnell Corporation

Section 14

Finding the Best Meeting Site

Finding just the right site for your sales meeting is perhaps one of the most important responsibilities in the entire planning process. It also can be one of the most frustrating, because everyone in the company probably has his or her own idea of what the ideal location is.

Since you are the one charged with choosing the site—and the one who has the fiscal responsibility to stay within the meeting's budget—the buck must stop with you.

Your first consideration will probably be the number of persons who will attend the gathering. The next will be the length of time allocated for the meeting and what type of meeting you require.

Narrowing down location

With your salespeople in mind, first ask yourself the following questions when picking a site:
- Where are most of your people coming from? Is geography a factor? Should the meeting be rotated among regions?
- Is night life a factor? Is sightseeing important? Should you choose an urban or resort setting?
- Will the salespeople be accompanied by spouses? Should the site be considered a jumping-off spot for tours or vacations?
- Is the site within the cultural framework of your salespeople's experience? Would they feel comfortable in the surroundings? If spouses will be present, is there enough to do during the day to keep them occupied?

It is also imperative that you ask yourself some questions about the gathering's purpose and general tone, such as:

©Dartnell Corporation

- What are the key objectives of your meeting? How will the site help to meet these objectives?
- Would it be best to hold the meeting at a location where there is little or no competition for your salespeople's attention, or is the meeting to be a combination of work and play?
- If exhibits are involved, is the site capable of accommodating them, and is it easily accessible for shipping? What is the labor situation at the site (if displays and exhibits are involved)?

Once you have settled these preliminary questions, it is time to go after the facts.

Convention and visitors' bureaus

Before making a personal on-site inspection of a specific property you may have heard about, contact the local convention or visitors' bureau in the areas you are considering. Ask for written information on transportation, hotels, convention halls, local services, shopping, tours, and cost advantages involved in off-season booking.

When requesting this information, make sure that you supply the convention bureau with a clear picture of your organization's sales meeting needs, including attendance, style of meeting, displays and exhibits, and range of dates for the meeting.

Some bureaus are excellent sources of assistance, especially when city officials, recognizing the value to the city of meeting business, have invested considerable municipal funds in making them excellent resources. It is well known that meeting attendees spend more money than do other categories of visitors, and cities are looking for a share of what has become a multi-billion dollar industry. Convention bureau staff members increasingly have honed their skills as the meeting/convention trade has boomed. Further, your best chances of getting objective answers to specific site problems will come from these people, who are selling an area, not a specific property. And they are interested in *total* attendance figures for the year, meaning that no business, however small it might seem to you, will be overlooked.

The convention bureau may have information about good independent hotels that might otherwise be overlooked. In most cases, convention bureaus also are able to provide room rates, information on access to and travel within the city, tickets to local sporting events, and so on. Many, when apprised of your meeting needs, will conduct site inspections. Some are willing to provide substantial support to corporate meetings in the form of promotional aids, registration assistance, badges, and so on. This varies with the location, but it is a resource often overlooked.

Visitors' bureaus in rustbelt cities are often extraordinarily helpful, as these cities look to replace heavy industry with increased meeting business. Not only do these cities typically have less expensive sleeping rooms and generally lower hotel expenses (bed and sales taxes are often only one-half that of some large cities), the cities themselves will often defray some of the costs of a meeting. Some have provided appropriate speakers and paid their fees in order to entice a meeting to their city. Cultivate as many contacts in local convention bureaus as you can, and ask to be put on their mailing lists.

The next step, if at all possible, is personal inspection of the site you have tentatively chosen. If this is not possible, ask the opinion of the salesperson or regional manager in that area. Chances are, they not only know the location, but may have been there recently. In this procedure, it is important not to rely too much on chance or second-hand opinions, even though the latter may sometimes be necessary for time and cost reasons.

Allow adequate lead time

All of this should be done far in advance of the actual meeting or convention, particularly if the meeting is a large one with elaborate displays and exhibits. A year's lead time is not unreasonable, considering the complexities involved. If the meeting is relatively small, your problems in sufficient lead time are minimized, but unless you are a steady customer of the site or a buddy of the manager, don't push your luck on nailing down the meeting location by waiting until the last minute. Remember, too, that most of the desirable site locations are chain-owned and -operated these days, meaning that they are highly computerized and far more cost-conscious than was the case even as recently as ten years ago.

Ask yourself the following questions during the site selection process. (This process of selecting a meeting site is covered in detail in Section 15.)

1. What is the general condition of the hotel and/or convention center?
2. Look at the hotel through the eyes of your salespeople. Are the rooms clean and well-furnished? Is the help efficient, clean, and courteous? Are the meeting rooms well-ventilated, properly lighted, and with enough stage and floor electrical outlets to handle your technical requirements?
3. How many meeting rooms are in the hotel? Are they free of pillars and other obstructions? What is the noise factor from outside these rooms?
4. Is the exhibit space adequate and properly lighted?
5. Are sleeping rooms comfortable?
6. How are the transportation facilities to and from the hotel? This has become most important recently because of the trend to build large hotels far from the center of most cities.
7. What facilities and services does the hotel supply? What is the availability of outside sources for other materials you will need?

Don't forget that the hotel you are negotiating with is just as eager as you to develop a smooth working relationship. Therefore, you should make a point of supplying the hotel manager with all possible information about your sales meeting.

This should include information about housing accommodations, your general time schedule (and whether you will need pre- and post-convention time), space requirements for meetings, exhibits, registration, service, ticket sales, and parking, plus servicing requirements, such as your program pattern for meals and other services.

This information will probably be requested by the hotel executive and, if it isn't, you will have your first clue that this particular hotel is not very experienced in handling meetings and conventions.

Determining price

Once you are near a decision on location, it is time to start talking about price. Have a meeting with the hotel executive and get probable room prices for your meeting. Make sure you determine at this time the price of all services involved in your meeting, such as rental of equipment, hauling fees, union work regulations, and anything else that can run up the basic costs in any way. Throughout this process, keep in mind that everything in the hotel or convention center business is negotiable.

A cooperative attitude on the part of hotel management is critical at any sales gathering. But cooperation is a two-way street, and it can be cultivated only by keeping in mind that the hotel must turn a profit on your gathering and that, if well run, the hotel will insist that its staff be treated with the same courtesies you demand from them.

Keeping a checklist

Figure 1 on page 142 presents a helpful checklist to keep at hand during your site selection process.

A lot of sales managers of your acquaintance probably keep checklists and will be happy to share them with you. But as volatile as the hotel business is these days, it is best to keep updating your information on possible sales meeting locations. Chain management of major hotels can bring on a certain uniformity throughout the industry, but it still depends on the skill and dedication of the local manager. This is particularly true when it comes to the attitudes and efficiency of the help.

Airport meeting sites

There are basically two types of airport hotels: those located within the airport terminal itself, such as at O'Hare Field, Chicago, and Miami International Airport, and those just outside the airport grounds.

The latter type are more popular and represent the vast majority of companies holding sales meetings at airport locations. In recent years, few new hotels have been built within terminal facilities, because of high costs and the reluctance of airport authorities to give up valuable space to a commercial venture that attracts even more people to an already congested area.

©Dartnell Corporation

Figure 1. Site Selection Checklist

Hotel (Center)_____ Address_____
Phone_____ Contact_____ Title_____
How many rooms_____ Rooms needed (Sleeping)_____
Rooms needed (Meeting)_____
How is transportation?_____
_____

How is parking?_____
_____

How is food service?_____
_____

Attitude of help_____
_____

What extras? (Welcoming party, exhibit set-ups, etc.)_____
_____

Shopping availability_____
_____

Tourist attractions_____
_____

Dates available_____
_____

Lead time required_____
Exhibit areas_____
_____

Local suppliers of equipment needed_____
_____

Date checked out_____

©Dartnell Corporation

Hotels just outside the airport gates are generally less expensive and usually have plenty of meeting rooms, especially for small groups. Airport meeting sites are used for a wide array of national and regional events, such as short training sessions, new product introductions, dealer/distributor meetings and, of course, sales meetings.

Advantages There are a number of benefits of using an airport location:

1. For a short meeting, your people can fly in and out the same day, thereby eliminating the cost of a sleeping room.
2. You'll save the time and expense (cab fares in particular) of traveling to a downtown or distant hotel.
3. Most airport hotels offer complimentary pick-up and return transportation.
4. Local people and those driving to the meeting are usually able to take major highways directly to the airport hotel.
5. Most airport hotels offer free parking, a further saving.

Disadvantages Airport hotels have some negatives, of course.

1. They usually do not have the amenities of a downtown or resort facility, although some of the newer, larger ones have indoor pools, exercise rooms, etc.
2. Since most guests are "captives" of the hotel, restaurants tend to be a bit pricey and sometimes have poor food and service.
3. Activity levels in these facilities are very high, with people frantically checking out to catch a plane. This may not be the ideal setting for a quiet, contemplative get-together!

Key points Here are some key points to keep in mind if you are considering holding a meeting at an airport hotel:

1. Advise participants far in advance how they should get from the airport to the hotel. Do they telephone the hotel for a pick-up or do they go outside the terminal and wait for a van?
2. If some people are driving, give them specific directions.
3. Let the attendees know in advance what facilities are available. Bringing the golf clubs could be a waste of time! Some sites have tennis courts, others do not.
4. Weekends are a slow time for airport hotels. If you can book

©Dartnell Corporation

your meeting for Saturday, you could get a better room rate.

5. If the meeting attendees will be staying for more than one night, it's best to plan some evening activity. You may want to schedule a group dinner, along with a speaker, or if you have a very large group, perhaps you should schedule entertainment after dinner.

6. Lock in your space early. Airport hotels book dozens of small meetings each week, so don't expect a tentative booking to hold for long.

Conference centers

The conference center has come into its own since 1975 and is gaining in popularity each year. There is no specific definition of a conference center, as opposed to a hotel that handles a lot of conferences, except as described by the International Association of Conference Centers (IACC).

IACC was founded a few years ago by a small group of conference center owners to try to improve the image of conference centers and to promote the concept. They felt that conference centers were getting a bad name, because a number of older hotels—especially resort hotels—were calling themselves conference centers in order to pick up some additional business, particularly in the slack season.

Conference centers have been around a long time, but were never popular with corporations and other organizations that hold a lot of meetings. Some were remote (some still are) and hard to reach; others were operated by universities and were quite spartan. The newer conference centers are as modern as any hotel, with most of the amenities.

Advantages

The primary benefits of holding a sales meeting at a conference center are:

1. Everything you need to run a meeting is available on the premises. This includes audio-visual equipment of most any variety or type. For example, closed-circuit television is available in all or most meeting rooms and sometimes in the sleeping rooms as well.

2. Staff members understand the business of meetings and, on the average, are more professional than a hotel staff.
3. Meeting rooms are designed for meetings, not general-purpose use. They usually have very comfortable chairs and excellent lighting and soundproofing.
4. Most are located in tranquil settings, which are conducive to quiet thought and contemplation. There are few distractions.
5. Small groups will usually get more attention from staff than in a hotel.
6. There is a better chance of controlling nighttime activity of attendees, since there's usually nowhere to go!
7. You will know your costs exactly, before the session starts.
8. There is some prestige connected to a conference center, particularly if it's part of a university or a well-known corporation. (Examples include University of Michigan, Ohio State University, MIT, Xerox Corporation.)

Disadvantages Some of the minuses of conference centers are:

1. Cost is usually higher. Conference centers must charge more, because they have no other source of revenue.
2. Contracts are more difficult to break, particularly for sleeping rooms. Associations and other organizations that are never sure of the exact number of attendees until the last minute should avoid conference centers, because of the tight guarantees that must be given. This is not a problem for corporations, because every meeting is a command performance and you'd better be there if you want to keep your job!
3. For a long meeting, some of your people may get a little stir-crazy—there's not much to do after dinner. This is particularly bothersome for salespeople, unaccustomed to hitting the books every evening from 7 to 10 p.m. It's best to have some evening activity planned, at least for one or two nights during the week.
4. Food can sometimes be a problem. Most conference centers offer a buffet for all three meals. Some people hate or can

©Dartnell Corporation

barely tolerate buffets. Some conference centers will provide a sit-down dinner at an additional cost, but there are always a few people who would rather go to a coffee shop and get a hamburger, which is not possible at a conference center. In fairness, both conference centers and hotels are becoming more flexible on offering special meals. Many people today are on diets and/or have excluded certain foods from their diets completely. One of the more common exclusions as of this writing is beef. This presents a major problem for any dining room serving group lunches and dinners, because beef continues to be the most popular main course in the United States, Canada, and Latin America.

5. Sleeping rooms may not be as plush or as comfortable as those in a top-notch hotel.

Added pros and cons

In talking with sales managers, training managers, and meeting planners, I've found there to be one overriding reason for their preference for conference centers: The facilities are conducive to learning. In their combined experience, managers and planners have found that the average student will learn more and retain more at a quiet conference center location.

Meeting professionals appreciate the fact that they can move into a meeting room on Sunday, have enough time to set everything up, and be ready to go on Monday morning. With extensive role-playing equipment, rear-screen and multi-screen equipment, simultaneous translation equipment and the like, they must be certain that the equipment can stay in place for the entire meeting. Because many corporations today run their sessions in the evenings as well as during the day, they will not and cannot move their equipment about just because the hotel needs the room for a wedding or a banquet.

Conference centers are particularly attractive for executive meetings. In recent years, the new conference centers have been built with tennis courts, racquetball courts, exercise rooms, saunas, jogging and hiking trails, indoor and outdoor swimming pools, and—sometimes—golf courses.

©Dartnell Corporation

Some sales managers and others responsible for meetings complain that the one total price per person per day does not fit in well with their meeting plans. For example, you will pay for three meals a day, whether you consume them or not. Many people skip breakfast. Sometimes the meeting planner wants to take the entire group out to a fine restaurant for dinner. Most conference centers charge for the dinner, whether it is eaten or not. These are some of the areas in which conference centers are inflexible. Because of this inflexibility, most meetings that require the participants to pay all or a part of the cost are not held at conference centers.

Some conference centers offer lower rates for guests arriving on Friday evening, with meetings on Saturday and Sunday, since this is usually a slow period.

Don't overlook the commercial and resort hotels that have built separate conference centers. These may well be the conference centers of the future, because they combine the best of traditional conference centers with the best of first-class hotels. The major hotel chains, including Marriott, are testing this type of dual operation as of this writing.

For more information on conference centers, contact The International Association of Conference Centers, 900 South Highway Drive, Fenton, MO 63026.

Section 15

Negotiating with Hotels

If your meeting is to be held on neutral ground, that is, away from the office, steel yourself for what can be fairly elaborate negotiating sessions with hotel managements. A seasoned sales manager we know once described this negotiation process as tap dancing with the flamingos. Few rules apply, and those that do can change from day to day and almost always from season to season.

Negotiations may be complicated further by how most hotels operate, with the left hand sometimes not knowing what the right hand is up to. The hospitality industry allots considerable authority to various staff executives. For example, the catering manager has an iron grip on food services, the room manager maintains an equally tight grip on sleeping and meeting rooms, and the general manager is in the middle, often in the role of mediator. The net result is that getting what you consider satisfactory accommodations and food at reasonable prices can be almost as difficult as getting an arms agreement out of Geneva.

As a meeting planner, the best way to approach negotiations with a hotel is to remember that things aren't always what they seem to be. Don't settle for the hotel's first offer, particularly if you have some obvious bargaining power, such as big numbers or a track record as a regular customer.

This is not to suggest that negotiations with hotel officials for your meeting should be conducted on an adversarial basis, an approach that will get you nowhere. Instead, let it be apparent from the outset that you are shopping around. Anyone who has shopped for a new car already knows some of the basic bargaining tactics.

©Dartnell Corporation

Obviously, you will be ahead of the game if you don't start your meeting-site shopping at the last minute. Hotel executives have a sure sense of your urgency. It is therefore important to get your meeting site nailed down in contract form as far in advance of the meeting as possible. In some of the most desirable locations, this can mean a year, or even more, in advance.

Find out, too, about such cost factors as seasonal rates or even days of the week that are less busy. Perhaps your best bargaining chip is the ability to be flexible as to date. There's no question that you'll get the best deal if you can book your meeting when the hotel needs the business, which is another reason for allowing lots of lead time in your planning. In some major cities such as New York, for example, weekends tend to be slow in the hotel trade. Good room bargains can be negotiated in such locations. The golden figure in hotel management is the weekly occupancy rate. To keep that figure as high as possible, management will make concessions on food and room prices or, as often happens, on compensatory services, such as a free hospitality suite, free meeting rooms, or free use of back-up equipment and set-ups.

Write a letter

If you have two or more hotels that you feel meet your requirements, you can save time—whether or not you have visited them for site inspection—if you write a similar letter to each outlining your exact needs, the dates of the sales meeting, and whether or not these dates are firm. In your letter you should state the kind of meeting you will be holding, the number of individuals attending, the number of sleeping rooms needed, meals, coffee breaks, meeting rooms, etc. You should then spell out what the minimum requirements of the hotel are in order for you even to consider it as a possible site. Some professional meeting managers find this an excellent tactic, because once the sales manager and hotel manager see the possibilities, they know to what extent they can negotiate.

Toward the end of the letter, you will state your minimum demands. For example, you might say, "In order for us to consider your hotel for our meeting, assuming that you have the space and rooms available, we will require the following services at no charge: 1) an opening first night reception with hot and cold hors d'oeuvres for 250 people; 2) all of our meeting rooms furnished at no charge; 3) one complimentary suite for the president of our company for three nights and two regular sleeping rooms for staff members, also at no charge, for three nights.

"If you are willing to provide these services, we will consider you for our meeting."

Even though the hotels may not agree to give you all the things you ask, they certainly will call you back, or write you, saying that they would like to talk about it further and perhaps make some of the concessions you requested. Of course, you must be careful not to ask for the world, but always ask for a little bit more than they would give you routinely. By employing this letter-writing tactic, your proposal will often be taken directly to the general manager of the hotel for his or her approval, whereas if you did not put your requirements in writing, the actual negotiations would take place when you visited the hotel. A letter is an excellent way to get a hotel's attention and point out the total amount of business and profit they can make from your function.

Get it in writing

In extracting hotel concessions—whether lower price or free services—make certain you get it all down in black and white. Your meeting naturally is the most important thing on your mind during negotiations, but remember that the manager you're dealing with probably has three or four gatherings pending with the same demands and problems.

Assuming you start early enough to have some bargaining chips, tackle one problem at a time. If at all possible, request an actual tour of the site, sleeping rooms, meeting rooms, dining rooms, kitchens, and lounges. Most general managers will be more than pleased to give you such a tour or assign someone to the task.

The next step usually is a session with the room manager, to whom you should outline the specific number of sleeping rooms and meeting rooms required, the dates of the meeting, and other requirements—such as lighting, props, and equipment for the sales sessions. Go into this meeting fully prepared and with specific numbers; stress certain requirements, such as sufficient space and soundproofing in meeting rooms. Some hotels have been known to scrimp on space in meeting rooms.

Who will your neighbors be?

It's always a good idea to find out what other groups will be using the hotel during your meeting. Having this information in advance of negotiating will tell you something about your competition for space. Some bookings are soft; that is, they have a higher than average chance of being cancelled, or they may simply be tentative bookings. Try to find out. Convention bookings, bookings by associations, and by other groups that can provide only an approximate number of attendees may also be considered soft bookings.

You should also consider the nature of the groups. Will your group be compatible with a group known for their all-night parties?

There is also the consideration of group size. If you have a small group and the remainder of the hotel is occupied by a single group, perhaps you will have difficulty getting the attention you need. Most meeting managers prefer a small hotel for a small group.

More and more hotels are offering space for exhibits and trade shows. This can be a big plus, if your organization is the one for which the show was developed. If not, it can be a major distraction. Some trade shows take on a carnival air. If your meeting room is nearby, it could be a problem for you. Of course, you can't consider every possibility, and you can't always know who will be using the meeting room next door.

This author remembers holding a three-day educational seminar at a very nice commercial hotel several years ago, utilizing one section of the ballroom. Although it was a fairly new hotel, the ballroom partitions were not soundproof. The balance of the ballroom was occupied by a fundamentalist religious group, which for three days and nights held a revival-type meeting, complete with organ music, group singing, preaching, and healing. To make matters worse, the entire lobby area outside the ballroom was filled with people

Negotiating with Hotels 153

hawking all types of religious articles. When we asked the hotel management to turn down the public address system in the adjoining room, he said, "I hate to tell you this, but they're not using any amplification!"

Be specific about your numbers

Be certain to have an accurate projection of the size of your meeting. Once you have contracted for a meeting room for 100, the hotel is under no obligation to provide a room for 150 if your numbers increase. Your number count is vitally important, because a meeting room appropriate for 100 is pretty cavernous when only 25 people show up. If you say 100 will attend a session, don't accept a room meant for no more than 50.

As your negotiations proceed from point to point, work from a checklist much like the one shown in Figure 1, below. When you

Figure 1. Checklist for Sleeping, Meeting and Hospitality Rooms

Totals

1. Number of sleeping rooms _____ @ $_____ $_____
2. Number of meeting rooms _____ @ $_____ $_____
   Size requirements _____ _____
                        (Size)   (Number)

                      _____ _____
                        (Size)   (Number)

3. Hospitality suite(s) _____ @ $_____ $_____
4. Banquet _____ @ $_____ $_____
   (Attendance #)

                                    Total $_____
                                          (Rooms)

Ask About

1. Room to be reserved for officers, program participants, special guests, etc. Give list of names and expected arrival and departure.
2. Complimentary rooms to be provided by hotel and whose will they be.
3. Billing arrangements.
4. Does hotel provide equipment needed? Free or charge? Give list of equipment needed.
5. Gratuity requirements.
6. Is there a mini-van or limo service to and from airport? Is it free? Frequency of pick-ups.
7. Hotel amenities such as pool, tennis courts, golf? What are fees?

©Dartnell Corporation

finish the checklist and have figures from the manager, go back over each one and question any figure that seems out of line or excessive. Your hesitation on some points can induce some compromises. Remember that the first quotes you get likely will be top of the line. Also, don't be hesitant to ask for extra services, or additional set-up assistance, etc. If the hotel is charging for the banquet meeting room, ask why. This room frequently comes at no charge, if you guarantee enough place settings.

Your next session probably will be with the banquet or catering manager. Go through much the same procedure as you did with the room manager. Be prepared with specifics: dates, times, place settings each day for breakfast, lunch, and dinner, cocktail or reception attendance, and food desired on each occasion. Don't just accept the first suggestion on menu items for an occasion without asking for alternatives. Here again, and quite naturally, the food manager will usually start off with the top of the line. If you've had the chance to eat in the hotel's public dining rooms, you will have a good fix on what the chefs keep in stock and can prepare in quantity. A menu built around these staples will save you big bucks at most hotels.

In discussing the cocktail party–reception segment, keep in mind that many food managers will provide free finger food if the guarantee is high enough. If you luck out on this, be sure to ask what the finger food will be and how it will be served.

Use the handy checklist shown in Figure 2, page 155, when negotiating with the food services or banquet manager.

Signing the contract

After you have concluded your negotiations with the room manager and catering manager (which may sometimes be concurrent), you'll have a final figure, the sum of all accommodations and services. This figure, if it is satisfactory, is then translated into a contract. Remember, if a deal seems too good to be true, it probably is. While everything—room rates, food and beverage, meeting and exhibit space, and even hotel-owned parking—is negotiable, you need to remember that the hotel also has its eye on the bottom line. It must make a profit on your group. Most big hotels have standard contracts,

©Dartnell Corporation

Figure 2. Checklist for Catering Functions

		Totals
1. Number of breakfasts	_____ @ $_____	$_____
2. Number of lunches	_____ @ $_____	$_____
3. Number of dinners	_____ @ $_____	$_____
4. Stocking hospitality suite	_____ @ $_____ (Days)	$_____
5. Number at banquet	_____ @ $_____	$_____
		$_____ (Total)

Ask About

1. Menu selections and price ranges. Price to include tax and gratuities.
2. Agree on time for final guarantee.
3. Time of servings.
4. Number at head table at banquet.
5. Lectern, microphone.
6. Billing procedures.
7. Cocktails. Free or cash bar? Cost per drink? Cutoff time, who makes it?
8. Flowers.
9. Place cards for head table.
10. Photographer for banquet.
11. Audio-visual set-ups?
12. Music arrangements.
13. Dressing rooms for entertainers.
14. Time allotted for each meal.
15. Press table, invitations at banquet.
16. Who will provide tickets, distribute them?

which should be studied carefully before you sign. You may wish to insist on a few additional paragraphs as the final step in the negotiation.

While all this sounds time-consuming and even complex, it is absolutely necessary—unless, of course, you are a firm believer in blind luck. The job of negotiating with hotel managements in this laborious way has been eased considerably in recent years by the huge growth of chain hotels, all of which maintain central offices in major cities for just such matters. However, this will depend on how much decentralization the chain believes in. Many chains, including some of the most successful ones, are firm believers in local autonomy. With other chains, you can handle your negotiations with the main office in much the same manner as you would do with individual managers.

Another factor to keep in mind is that most major hotels in recent years have started free airport pick-up and return service with mini-vans operated by the hotel. Considering taxi fares in most locations, use of this service can result in substantial savings. It is your responsibility to let those arriving for your meeting know of the service and how to connect with it.

Another critical consideration, before signing the contract, is to ask what kind of audio-visual equipment the hotel or convention site can supply. Asking for a chalkboard or screen doesn't guarantee a usable chalkboard or screen. The hotel people frequently feel that they have met their end of the bargain when they have put up something in the room that resembles a screen or chalkboard. They are not audio-visual experts. It's a good idea to look at the available equipment *before* the day of the meeting. The same holds true for projection equipment, which always should be inspected the night before the meeting. Make it clear to the hotel people that you intend to run this check.

It is a good idea, too, not to put all your eggs in one basket in booking space for your meeting. Try to investigate and price out at least two locations acceptable to your needs. You might be surprised at the wide price differentials, even between comparable facilities. This all depends, of course, on the aggressiveness of hotel management and how eager they are to burnish that golden figure—the weekly occupancy rate.

In the course of all these negotiations, you doubtless will get to know more about the mysteries of hotel management than you care to. However, you also are likely to strike up lively friendships with some hotel professionals, thereby establishing contacts that can stand you in good stead in the future. Make no mistake—hotel professionals today are a sharp bunch. Because of the nature of their

©Dartnell Corporation

business, they have seen and heard nearly everything. Treated with respect and consideration, they will respond and not infrequently share with you some of their knowledge of how their system operates. This knowledge can be invaluable in knowing how far you can go and how many extras you can get by merely asking.

Hotel professionals, too, are a tightly knit community. They know competitive factors, and they frequently can be a good source of inside information on how the hotels in the area are making out on their occupancy figures. In other words, cultivate hotel contacts if you use off-site facilities for meetings. A couple of good hotel contacts can save you hours of frustration in the future.

Booking entertainment

If you have good rapport with the hotel managers you are dealing with, it generally is a good idea to seek their advice in booking and organizing the entertainment sections of your program. Major hotels work all the time with entertainment packagers or booking agents. They know the prices and even who is in town and available. Some hotels even have arrangements with entertainment packagers and can handle this segment of the program, along with providing rooms and food services. (Booking entertainment is discussed at length in Section 21.)

Setting up credit

Your hotel contact will probably not be a bit shy about inquiring how your bills will be settled, but if he or she doesn't mention it, you must. Your credit must first be established with the hotel. You will provide references in the usual fashion.

Your bill will be in several parts. There will be group charges, including items such as meeting rooms, group meals and cocktail parties, and any equipment rented from the hotel. Each sleeping room will have a separate account. It is critical at this point to decide what your company is going to pay for. Perhaps it will assume charges for room and tax only, leaving meeting attendees responsible for incidental charges, such as room service, laundry, and so on. Perhaps the company will pay whatever is charged to the room, billing the attendee for unauthorized expenses. A third way is to have each attendee provide a major credit card imprint upon check-in. He or she is then billed for the expenses charged to the room and submits an expense report to the company for reimbursement following the meeting. This decision should be made at the time the contracts are signed for the meeting; it will vary from one company to another. Do not assume, however, that just because your firm is large and well known, credit will automatically be extended by the hotel. The method of payment must be determined at the time the meeting is planned.

In summary   Perhaps the single most important factor in choosing a hotel is to determine how badly they want your business. This may be difficult to tell in advance, since hotel managers make their livings by being gracious to people. What you really need to know is the amount of action and service you will get.

Remember, hotels are not designed for any one specific purpose, including your own. They cater to all kinds of businesses and individuals and, consequently, almost always have something going on.

It is not possible to overstate the importance of checking out a hotel site in advance to look for such things as stale air, full ashtrays, etc. After deciding on the facility, it is a good idea to learn the names of the head maintenance person, the head housekeeper, and the desk captain. These are the people who make the place run or falter. If professional, they also know the importance of the word "hospitality" in their jobs.

Section 16

Opening the Meeting

The room is ready. Everyone is seated. You've got all your ducks in a row. The lights go up. You're on! But are you really ready to open the meeting?

What you do in the first few minutes of any sales meeting is critical to the meeting's overall success. What you are dealing with is a fragile human emotion: *anticipation*. Everyone in the room is looking forward to what is ahead. You can increase and heighten that anticipation by concentrating in advance on a good, strong beginning.

A positive tone of voice is the first requirement in a strong opening, coupled with a professional air in both demeanor and appearance. It's no accident that successful cabaret and nightclub performers capture their audiences in the first few minutes of their acts. The opening should be an upbeat preview of what's to come. Don't give it all away, but quickly define the purposes of the meeting and how you intend to accomplish these purposes.

The question technique always seems to be effective in this type of opening. Ask rhetorical questions as you go along, such as, "Are we going to allow Brand X to dominate shelf space in favor of our Brand Y?" "Why aren't we?" "We'll learn why during the course of this meeting." Base your rhetorical questions on actual concerns within the firm—ones you know are lurking in the backs of the minds of the sales personnel. This opening technique alerts the audience to what's ahead and heightens anticipation.

Every meeting, especially the kind that comes about regularly, has its own set of priorities, which set the tone of the gathering.

One meeting might be critical to increasing sales or to increasing morale after some setback; another meeting might be aimed at how to resist the temptation to coast, after some startling successes in the market. Each meeting has its own overpowering dynamic, which should be identified in your opening. You must set the tone of the meeting right off the bat. Always lead from strength.

There are any number of ways to open meetings, to introduce speakers, and to involve the salespeople in the proceedings from the beginning. For example, you might consider having on hand a member or two of the top management team to welcome attendees as they arrive. (If they will stay to visit informally during the first coffee break, so much the better.) Try to provide an old hand to act as a buddy to a first-timer. Be sure you have enough staff on hand to serve as ushers.

Following are some time-tested methods for getting things off to a rousing start.

Ice breakers

Ice breakers set the pace for everything that follows. However, if you are not cautious in their use, you risk creating a hostile or cold atmosphere.

Here are some ideas:

1. Hand out a name tag to each salesperson, making sure the person gets the wrong tag. The members of the audience then must search the room for the person who has his or her name tag. This is an effective method of getting people to know one another in a hurry.
2. Cut pictures in half and paste on name tags. Individuals must then find the other half of their picture and sit next to that person at the next meal. This is another fast method of breaking up cliques that tend to develop at sales gatherings.
3. Put a letter from the firm's name on each participant's name tag. Tell the group they must get together with others to spell out the firm's name.
4. Have your people pass around fake money on which they must write a meeting idea. Explain that the moral is that while the exchange of money doesn't enrich anyone, an idea exchange enriches everyone.

©Dartnell Corporation

Introductions

If your sales meeting is relatively small, or if you have broken the group into work units right after the opening remarks, rely on introductions to get things off and running. The thing to guard against here, however, is allowing self-introductions to descend into either horn-blowing or self-conscious embarrassment.

Techniques that can overcome this are:
- Tell the group that all will have a couple of minutes to think about a successful experience in their lives, which they then will use in introducing themselves to the group. Then allow each person one or two minutes to make the self-introduction.
- After three minutes, slips of paper are passed around, with each person receiving one slip for every other member. After each self-introduction, each person will write on one of the slips a word or phrase that best sums up the outstanding characteristic of the speaker. Everyone folds the slips of paper and passes them to the podium. Then the next speaker takes over.
- After everyone has made his or her self-introduction, pass out 3 x 5 cards and ask each person to write at the top of the card, Personal Power Base.
- Next, the speaker goes through all the slips of paper and calls out the most commonly mentioned qualities that group members have detected in one another. In most cases you will be pleasantly surprised to find that most of your group admire the same qualities.
- Ask that each person write down the qualities most commonly rated as outstanding among the group. Then ask each person to add to that list as the meeting moves along, whenever he or she detects an outstanding quality in another person at the meeting.

Values session

This is an effective way to shortcut the sometimes too-lengthy time needed for self-introductions and follow-ups. It amounts to breaking your group into units of two or three and asking members of each unit to briefly interview one another about the one value he or she considers the most important. Then ask each group to interact with another group, asking the same questions after each person has been introduced to one another. This procedure will produce lively conversation. It is a good method of getting each participant to understand that values change from person to person, and that it is important to be receptive to the needs and values of others.

Stunts and gimmicks

When used with discretion, this technique can be an effective means of opening the sales session. However, do not let the showman in you dominate. Use this technique only to make a serious point, rather than solely for entertainment value. Avoid subtle stunts or elaborate gimmicks and don't overdo the stunt routine.

Here are a couple of stunts that can be pulled off easily and that dramatize a point you might want to make.

- To show the value of work, stick dollar bills at random on the bottoms of some chairs in the meeting room. At the right moment (usually during a lull), ask everyone to look at the underside of their chairs. A buzz will soon go through the room as those who have discovered cash under their seats make that fact known.

  Then say something like, "This demonstrates better than mere words that a good salesperson has to get off his or her seat to make a buck."

- To show your salespeople how allowing a customer to talk can defuse objections, take an inflated balloon with the word *objection* printed on it. Then let some air out of the balloon in bursts, so that the word "objection" becomes less and less noticeable. Finally, allow the balloon to deflate completely. The point you make is that the more the customer cites objections, the more the objection itself is deflated. The moral, of course, is that salespeople should resist the urge to interrupt the buyer's litany with rebuttals.

- Use a heckler, but sparingly, to stress points during the opening. Try to plant the word you know will be going through the minds of the salespeople in the heckler's diatribe.

©Dartnell Corporation

This is a good way to achieve a mind-set in the audience, when stressing a key point.

Advance assignments

An extremely effective method of getting peak interest in the meeting—even before it starts—is to give out pre-meeting assignments to the salespeople. This is also one of the easiest ways to provide participants with knowledge of what the meeting will be about. Best of all, it makes each participant a contributor to the total meeting effort.

Here are some effective advance assignment ideas.
- Have salespeople come prepared to pitch competitive products. This is especially useful in training on how to overcome objections.
- Mail out case histories which contain problems for your group to solve and return to you before the meeting.
- Outline a selling plan of action in advance and ask your people to try it out. Let them know that their experience with the plan will be discussed at the meeting. You will thus have no time lag in evaluating the new method and you will gain valuable pre-meeting involvement.
- Distribute questionnaires prior to the meeting, asking the salespeople to evaluate the organization in terms of its reputation in such areas as product quality, service, quality of servicing of accounts, management, delivery schedules, customer relations, or any other pertinent aspect of your firm's operations.
- Assign some of your people to spots on the program.
- Ask salespeople to note what problems their customers discuss with them the most. Ask them to keep a record and to make a report at the meeting. This can also be done with the most common customer complaints, although it is best to hold off until after the opening on this; you'll generally hear plenty on the topic as the meeting goes along.

It is difficult to generalize on what techniques will be effective openers at any meeting. Each industry has its own folklore, its own jargon, and its own level of presumed dignity. Some of the opening techniques that would work, say, at a meeting of apparel salespeople, would go over with a thud at a meeting of stockbrokers.

Whatever the group's primary sales interest, it is essential to kick off the gathering with a strong opening, keeping in mind the following:

Do
- Start on a positive note.
- Set the tone immediately.
- Plan as much pre-meeting involvement as possible.
- Use the past tense sparingly.

Don't
- Use stunts that are overly subtle.
- Make negative references to competitors.
- Allow the opening to run on too long or drift.

Section 17

Making a Presentation

In terms of a sales meeting, the difference between a speech and a presentation is the difference between night and day.

A speech is normally devoid of any props or visuals; by definition it is a verbal exercise. A presentation is a combination of the verbal *and* visual, with as much emphasis as is logical on the visual. In a sense, a presentation is show and tell. An effective presentation is usually far more difficult to bring off than a speech, for a presentation must illustrate what you are saying at the time you say it and this, if nothing else, requires more than normal mental agility.

The goal of any presentation is effective communication. This is nothing more than getting your message across as simply as possible. To achieve this goal, it is necessary to have in mind the results you desire from the audience. The nature of these results determines your selection of germane resource materials.

At the core of an effective presentation is meaningful content, without which your presentation is nothing. No number of gimmicky presentation aids will overcome a basic lack of content. It should be remembered—but too often is not—that a presentation is not a vaudeville act. A presentation's purpose is to define and educate, not to entertain.

Types of presentations

There are a variety of presentations, the most common being the following.

1. *Persuasion*. While all presentations should contain an element of persuasion, one designed specifically to persuade should achieve the following:

©Dartnell Corporation

- Pique the interest of the sales force in a new service, product, or technical advance you may be offering
- Gain the sales force's confidence in the organization you all represent
- Convince members of the sales force of the need for changes in operating procedures, commission rates, territories, etc.

The easiest of these to bring off in a presentation is the creation of interest in a new product. Here you are dealing in specifics and you have something exciting to show—the new product itself. It is a tougher act to persuade a group about the need for territory changes or other company policies that may be contemplated. Here you must work hard to have the most convincing visual back-ups you can assemble.

2. *Explanatory.* This method of presentation relies less on specifics than the one that sets out to persuade. You're after the broad picture here and should avoid nitty-gritty detail as much as possible. This type of presentation might be used for the following occasions:

- To orient new employees as to who's who and what's what within the organization
- To explain the opening of a new factory or distribution point and what this means to the individual salespeople
- To outline to the sales reps the particular needs and problems of another division of the company

The explanatory presentation is easier to organize, usually, than the persuasive type. For example, your presentation to new employees can and probably should include introduction of people in other departments with whom the neophytes will be dealing on a day-to-day basis.

3. *Teaching.* Here you instruct your audience on how to use some new piece of equipment or how to conform to some new company policy regarding paperwork (new computer system, for example).

Several uses for this type of presentation are:

©Dartnell Corporation

- To teach sales reps how a new product works and what its advantages are
- To teach the sales force why it is so important to get along with the new computer system by marking the right boxes and using the correct codes on order forms, etc.
- To coach sales personnel on specifics of behavior that will increase productivity

4. *The Oral Report.* This generally is an update on an ongoing program or policy. You can use some detail but also should assume that most of your audience is familiar with your subject. Some applicable uses are:
   - To bring the sales force up to date on a new building project or a new packaging program from the last sales meeting
   - To inform top management of how current expenditures on a program match with the budget
   - To inform all the reps of the progress being made by a study group or committee appointed to tackle a company problem of common interest

The importance of practice

Reading this section will not make you a good speaker or presenter, unless you have natural talent. Speakers get to be good from a combination of things. They must have something useful and interesting to say and must deliver those useful and interesting ideas with belief, enthusiasm, and vigor. This may sound easy, but it can be difficult for a variety of reasons, not the least of which is lack of practice. Add to that a basic fear of speaking which, while not fatal, may end up making your audience so nervous they may think it would be a mercy if you would just drop dead on the spot!

Looking at it from the positive side, you need only to be "pretty good" to be better than most sales managers. Sales managers are outstanding in front of a customer, but put them in front of a group, even one made up of their own people, and they more often than not turn into mumbling, bumbling bowls of jelly! However, with a little planning and a little practice, you will have those butterflies in your stomach flying in formation.

©Dartnell Corporation

When you see or hear a professional speaker, you may be in awe and not thinking about the fact that the same speech was delivered to hundreds of audiences, almost word-for-word as you're hearing it. Why shouldn't the speaker be good? With that many tries, the talk has been polished over and over again—a word added, perfect pauses, and gestures that are now second-nature all adding up to a masterpiece.

You could do the same, but you don't have the time. Instead, you should plan and organize your talk just as the professional speaker does, and then practice it as much as you can, with the bulk of the practice as close to the time of the speech as possible.

If your talk is planned out a month before you are scheduled to deliver it, practice it only enough at that time to make sure it's about as you want it. Have someone videotape your presentation so that you can review the tape several times, making changes you think are needed. If possible, keep taping each successive run-through, polishing as you go along. Ask your family or your fellow workers to review the tapes with you, so that you can have their perspective.

Here's a warning about the advice of others: unless they know you and your personality, as well as the intended audience, you may get some poor advice. Here's why. They will tend to put themselves in your place, with their comments reflecting how they would deliver your speech. Nevertheless, they are not you and you would be wise to ignore those suggestions that would have you saying their words in their style.

One of the first things a professional speech coach will tell you is to be yourself. If you're a mean old curmudgeon in everyday life, then be a mean old curmudgeon when you stand before your group. Let's face it, they expect it of you!

A marketing director I used to work with was a stickler about having everyone who was on the program at the annual national sales meeting practice his or her speech the night before going on stage, until the speech was just right. Roughly translated, that meant that you had to do it to his satisfaction.

This person would stay up all night with you until your speech was perfect. While almost everyone hated him for it the night before,

©Dartnell Corporation

they thanked him when the presentation was over the next day. The company president, after sitting through an entire day of presentations, said, "I'm amazed at how professional all of you have become since I last heard you speak." What he didn't know was that most of us had been up most of the night before practicing over and over again!

Take every opportunity to give a speech. Don't worry about who's in the audience—practicing before a group is the important thing. Keep the best parts of each speech and try to use them again. Every professional speaker does. Some thoughts are so generic that they're appropriate at most any time. Here's an example—the idea that you should never give up on a goal that's really important to you. Literature is filled with stories of individuals who never gave up and finally succeeded—the immigrant, the athlete, the student.

Everyone knows these stories. If you've been talking to your troops about pushing a product into the best-seller slot, and you've been trying unsuccessfully for some years to do so, this success story fits perfectly into your presentation. It doesn't matter that the audience has heard the story before, not even if they've heard it from you. If they know that you believe it can be done, then there's a good chance that they, too, will believe it. If the purpose of your talk is to persuade, then you've accomplished your mission.

Developing the presentation

Step one: Planning

Assuming you've decided on the topic, you should sit down with a pencil and paper and do a little planning. Your talk should have a clear purpose. Ask yourself, What do you want to happen as a result of what you're going to say or present? Let's say, for example, that your goal is to motivate the salespeople in the audience to make a minimum of two cold calls every day. Assuming this can be done given the time constraints they face, then what you have on your hands is a job of persuasion.

A good question to ask at this point is, "What can I say that will persuade them to make the cold calls?" Make a list, such as
1) benefits they will receive (increased commissions, etc.); 2) ways for

them to do it (example, telephoning); 3) training we can provide; 4) call aids we can provide; 5) positive reinforcement we can use.

I'm sure you can think of more, but now you have the nucleus of the persuasive information and ideas you're going to present.

Step two: The outline

The outline is the foundation on which you will develop your talk. It puts things in the order you want to say them. After a little thought, and particularly after your first practice, you may decide to rearrange your points a bit.

Your outline should be no more than two pages long. You just want to capture the key points right now. At the top of the page, write out your goal(s), so they will be in front of you as you're developing the outline.

Then break down your content into three parts—opening, body of the talk, and conclusion. Start with the body of your talk and list each main point you wish to make. When this is completed, start listing subpoints under each main point. For example:

Main point:	Talking with prospect via phone prior to a personal visit will make the personal visit easier.
Subpoint:	Here's what you should say to the prospect when you telephone.
Minor Subpoint:	Here's how to get past the secretary, in order to talk with the prospect via the telephone.

The benefit of using the point/subpoint technique is that it holds the attention of the audience and keeps you from rambling or spending too much time on minor points. A subpoint should support a main point. Subpoints can be examples, statistics, testimonials, comparisons, quotations, and the like. If you've ever been involved in debating, you will see the similarity with making a speech.

Guard against too detailed an outline to start. Stick with the key points. You can always expand your outline later. Use key words and phrases, such as, more sales, more dollars; 30 minutes a day; warming cold calls, etc. Your final outline can be a bit more detailed. But remember, if you're going to work from notes when you give your speech, it's much better to work from a few key trigger words than from a lengthy outline.

Once you've outlined the body of your talk, move to the opening or introduction. We'll cover the body of the speech later in this section. Remember that the introduction sets the stage for the body of your speech. It should be short and to the point, taking no more than 10 to 15 percent of your total speech time. A 30-minute speech should have a 3- to 4-minute opening.

Make the opening forceful and let it set the tone for the balance of your talk. Go slowly. Relax. Don't say too many things. Speak at a somewhat slower pace than you will when you get to the body of your talk. Here's where you establish rapport.

As you develop your outline, remember that the opening needs to:
1. Immediately gain attention
2. Establish rapport
3. Create a mood—serious, upbeat, contemplative, etc.
4. Explain the purpose
5. Develop expectations
6. Describe benefits

A good opening contains one or more of the following elements:
1. States a problem
2. Offers a solution
3. Asks one or more questions
4. Expresses an opinion
5. Offers a compliment
6. States a challenge
7. Tells a story
8. Describes what is to come
9. Relates to a current situation
10. Is dramatic

The last thing you say in the opening should flow smoothly into the body of your talk, so that the audience is unaware of the transition.

Now your outline is complete, except for your final remarks or conclusion. The conclusion should be even shorter than the opening—2 or 3 minutes is about right. Some speakers say, "and now in conclusion," and then talk on and on while the audience wonders if they will ever conclude!

First of all, never use the phrase, "and now in conclusion." Also, never apologize for taking so much of their time. Do let them know that you are winding up, however. You might say, "Let me review the key points here" or, "The final and most important point to be made is—."

Never go back over *every* point you covered. Do not summarize what you've said, but rather summarize or state for the first time what you want the audience *to do* as a result of listening to you. If you're requesting that they do something, now's the time to say it. Be specific. Tell them what you want them to do and when they should do it. Quickly state the key benefits they will receive if they do as you ask; and if they have been a good audience, tell them.

Know what your final words will be. They do not need to be dramatic or earth-shaking. They could simply be, "With your support, next year will be our best yet" or, "The future looks bright for our new line of lingerie." It's not likely that your *final* parting words will be remembered for more than a few seconds, unless you say, "Now let's all go to lunch!"

How to practice your speech

The benefits of practice are rather obvious—becoming familiar with the material, becoming less dependent on your notes, etc. There are other benefits as well. Practice enables you to:

1. Add "polish"
2. Uncover problem areas
3. Improve timing
4. Make yourself more comfortable
5. Increase your confidence

Perhaps the last point above is the most valuable—increasing your confidence. If you receive no other benefit, it would be worth the extra time to practice. Here are some tips on rehearsing:

1. Time each practice session. Anticipate time needed for questions.
2. Get the thoughts of several people. If your audience will be salespeople, find salespeople to listen to you rehearse. Their comments will be most valuable.

©Dartnell Corporation

Making a Presentation 173

3. If possible, practice your speech in the same room as it will be delivered, using the same props, lectern, audio-visual aids, public address system, etc. If this is not possible, simulate the setting as nearly as you can.

4. Videotape your presentation and review the tape immediately, then run through your speech again.

5. If you're going to be introduced, practice that, too. At least practice what you will say, if anything, about or to the person introducing you.

6. Make notes to yourself immediately after each run-through as to what you want to change or say differently.

7. If you're using an outline or cue cards, change them as you go along.

8. If you will be working with a projectionist, stage manager, or other individuals, practice with them, if possible. It will make their job easier and make you look more professional.

9. Leave nothing to chance. Check every prop, every slide, and each piece of equipment you'll be using.

10. Make your final practice session as close to the actual time of presentation as you can. If you're on at 10 a.m., practice at 9 a.m.

How to deliver your speech

There are a few important points to remember when you deliver a speech. The Toastmasters Club or any speech class usually mentions a number of key points, a discussion of which follows.

Eye contact

Let everyone in the room know that you're looking their way frequently. Move your gaze to one area of the audience and keep it there for about ten seconds. Then move to the next section and repeat. Rhythm and timing are important. Don't move your head too quickly and don't continue to repeat the same pattern.

Constant reference to your notes and visuals is distracting to the audience. Look at your notes only when necessary and when you do, be sure it's at a time when a natural pause occurs. When you're pointing at a chart or screen, find your place on the chart or screen, then turn to your audience when you speak. Unless you have voice

©Dartnell Corporation

amplification, it will be difficult for the audience to hear you when you're facing in the opposite direction.

Never, never read a speech

It will drive your audience up the wall. If there is a portion of your talk that needs to be very specific, such as a new pricing policy, you can say, "I'm going to read our new pricing policy, because I don't want to leave anything out. Listen carefully, so you will understand it." You can use visuals to help you remember what you're going to say, so you never need to read or even refer to your notes. In fact, some speakers work strictly from visuals, such as a flip chart or overhead projector, basically putting their speech outline on the screen, one or two points at a time. One caution here: Don't leave anything on the screen or chart unless you're constantly referring to it. If you're talking apples and your screen shows oranges, it is both distracting and confusing to the audience. If you want to keep good eye contact and hold attention, turn off the projector or cover the flip chart when you're not using it. Some professional speakers have a rule that they will never project an image for more than one minute. It's a good rule, although to follow it, you will need to put only a few words or images on each panel. The same effect can be achieved on an overhead projector by using a mask to cover a portion of your material.

Using pauses

Comedians are masters of the pause, waiting for the audience to laugh. We can learn a lot from how they "milk" the audience for every chuckle.

Using pauses is difficult, because most of us do not use them in our normal day-to-day conversation. They are necessary when speaking to a group, because not everyone finishes their listening at the same time! If you're making an important point, pause for a moment when you're finished, to let it sink in. Pausing also provides valuable time for you to think about what you will say next or glance at your notes. Pausing adds drama, as well as helping you separate the various portions of your talk. Of course, your pauses should appear deliberate, otherwise the audience may think that you can't figure out what you're going to say next.

Use the pause in the following circumstances:

©Dartnell Corporation

1. Before answering a question
2. When moving from one thought to another
3. Before and immediately after making a key point
4. After asking a rhetorical question
5. Before and after summarizing.

Let them know you're alive

Here we can take a lesson from the TV evangelist. He (or she) never stands still, is always moving about the stage, and occasionally points skyward, which may have more impact on the audience than the words being spoken. While you may point skyward only when mentioning the president of your company or your largest customer, you will learn a lot about presentation techniques by watching TV on Sunday morning.

A lectern or podium is a handy place to keep your notes and your watch. That's about all. Otherwise avoid it like the plague. Some speakers think the podium is a good place to hide, so that no one can see anything but their heads! If you feel that way, it's better not to speak at all. You've got to get out there and rub shoulders with the troops. Don't be afraid that your fly is unzipped or that you have a run in your pantyhose. First of all, very few in the audience will notice or care, particularly if you have something of interest to say.

Second and more important, you must get close to the audience, both physically and mentally. This is not likely to happen when you stand motionless behind a lectern or never move from one spot.

Stand up straight, yet appear relaxed but not too casual. After all, you are the star attraction. Keep your hands out of your pockets and gesture frequently to make a point or to provide emphasis. Right-handed people tend to overuse their right hands in gesturing and vice versa. Be aware of this and alternate from one hand to another.

Avoid the overuse of any one gesture. Instead, select the gesture to fit the point you're making. For example, use a clenched fist when you want to indicate strength or solidarity, fingers extended when you refer to numbers, and an upward palm when you refer to rising sales. In other words, the gesture must fit the point. Gestures are especially effective when expressing emotion and intensity. Gestures and actions to avoid include:

1. Pointing your finger at the audience
2. Placing your hand in your pocket
3. Smoking or chewing gum
4. Playing with a pointer or other prop
5. Straightening your tie or fiddling with your clothing
6. Rubbing your chin or drumming your finger

Letting them know you're alive can be aided by using the proper pitch and tone of voice. Most people do not have the kind of voice that will make them acceptable to a TV network or to a Shakespearean company. A lot of us have voices that do not project naturally and do not carry beyond the first few rows of the audience. Without amplification, we will not be heard unless we project our voices intentionally. This takes practice, but it can be aided by deeper breathing and projecting the voice from the diaphragm, as well as by speaking more slowly.

The loudness of your voice should vary from a whisper to a shout, depending on what you're saying at the moment and to focus attention at critical junctures. Increase the volume when you want to stir the audience, show excitement, or ask a thought-provoking question. Lower your voice when you want to make a contrasting point, express sympathy or concern, or for dramatic or emotional effect. Don't speak too softly, for the audience may not be able to hear you.

Unless you normally speak at a very rapid rate, address the audience at your normal rate or a little bit slower. If you make good use of the pause mentioned above, you'll be in good shape. If you speak rapidly as a general rule, and particularly if you tend to run your words together or drop your voice at the end of a sentence, you will frustrate your audience. The only known cure for this ailment is to slow down and enunciate those words that you know from past experience have been hard for a listener to understand. Regional accents can be particularly bothersome, unless of course your audience hails from the same part of the country. A midwesterner, for example, will have difficulty understanding a rapidly speaking Bostonian. On the other hand, the Bostonian may have no trouble at all understanding the midwesterner.

Speech content: the body

As a sales manager, you may have little choice as to the subject matter of your speech. If sales are off on the put-out-to-pasture products, you're going to have to talk about it (especially if your boss is in the audience)! On the other hand, you can make just about any topic interesting if you work at it. Speech content should be well organized and concise, easy to understand, and delivered with some conviction. How do you do that when you have to talk about the put-out-to-pasture line?

First: Set Some Priorities. That may best be done by deciding what you don't want to say. Reciting the history of the older products and how the founder of your company made the first batch in the basement of his tiny little house in East Snowshoe, Montana, may not be the best place to start. Instead, talk about recent history and that small core of steady users that, if expanded slightly, will put your company on the road to wider distribution and increased profits.

Second: Develop Your Talk Around One Central Theme.

Third: Limit Your Main Points to 5 or 6. If you absolutely must cover more points, bunch them together. For example, if you want to cover 15 critical issues facing your company next year, try grouping related issues together, reducing the number of main points from 15 to perhaps 5. Two or 3 may be financial issues, 3 or 4 may be customer issues, etc.

Fourth: Sort Your Material. When you're reviewing your material before developing a speech outline, sort it into three groups: critical information (must cover); important (should cover); and interesting information (if time allows). By doing this quick sort, you'll avoid the common problem of too much material and too little time. The details can always be covered in a handout.

Fifth: Make the Content Easy to Understand. The 5 or 6 main points should not be complex. State them in terms your audience will understand and be sure they stand out from the other things you say. Avoid technical jargon. Be clear. Use stories, analogies, definitions, examples, and illustrations to improve comprehension and understanding.

©Dartnell Corporation

Sixth: Make the Speech Interesting. That's sometimes difficult. You have to work at it. You can do this by getting audience participation, using skits, offering humor, telling interesting stories, making shocking or controversial statements (be careful here), and asking soul-searching questions. Using props and audio-visual materials will also help.

One professional speaker I know uses anything at hand to make a point—today's newspaper (the world's going to hell again), the American flag over in the corner (hard work is what keeps our flag flying, so why don't you in the audience help the cause), or the clothing styles present (is our thinking as modern as our dress?). You can do the same.

A well-known publisher who occasionally gives speeches uses a similar technique that's very effective. He has a large table placed on stage, close to the audience. On this table will be 10 or 15 objects, each one to be used during his talk. A typical list of items includes several newspaper and magazine clippings, a large bottle of aspirin, a shoe box, a pair of handcuffs, an apple, a cane, a videocassette, and a large photograph of Christopher Columbus.

In his opening remarks, he never mentions that table or items and, in fact, never looks at them. As his speech progresses and he wants to make a key point, he will walk to the table, pick up the item that helps him make the point, and hold it up. For example, he will pick up the handcuffs and say, "Are you wearing these handcuffs right now by not allowing yourself to consider a better way to sell?" When he's made that point, he puts the handcuffs back on the table and goes on to the next point. Later he will pick up a newspaper editorial and read it: "The editor of the New York Times says, 'This country will never achieve greatness until it can reduce its spending and balance its budget, etc., etc.'" After reading several paragraphs, the speaker will stop and say, "Some beliefs never change. This editorial was written fifty years ago." He then goes on to say that while important people are making gloom and doom predictions, the country continues to develop, solve problems, and make economic progress.

©Dartnell Corporation

You, too, can use the props-on-the-table technique quite effectively. It has a twofold effect of creating anticipation and greatly increasing recall. Try it.

Seventh: Develop Rapport. Start by covering points of mutual interest and agreement before bringing up points that may be controversial or unpopular. Use stories and examples with which the audience can identify. Refer to people who are liked and admired by the audience and tie them to your points. Use positive statements.

Avoid reference to anything that would threaten or embarrass anyone, particularly those in the audience. Don't preach, make threats, use profanity, or make sexist or racial remarks. Rather, build on good will and common interest. Above all, be of good cheer and smile as much as you can or as seems appropriate. Have a little fun, but be sure to make jokes about yourself, not others.

Eighth: Be Convincing. That may be difficult if you're not entirely convinced yourself. Nevertheless, you must try just as hard to convince your salespeople to use that new, more complex reporting form as you do when you want them to do a bang-up job of introducing a new product. Selling a new idea to your sales force is not much different than selling to a customer. Talk features and benefits, explain the product or service, and get the customer (your salespeople) involved. You will certainly want to make proof statements (test market results, taste tests, etc.). Select material that will support your idea or proposal. Offer alternatives—you can present the new products to your customers in one of several ways.

Before trying to convince anyone of anything, you need to put in a little thought. Think about the questions that will be raised and the concerns that will be expressed. Think about specific individuals in the audience, especially the influential ones. What will their reactions be?

An audience will generally notice if you have carefully considered the main points and taken their possible concerns into account *before* you talk with them. This means a lot to an audience and to your salespeople. Being concerned and thoughtful never goes out of style.

©Dartnell Corporation

How to say it best

So far we've talked mostly about *how* to give an effective presentation, but little about the words themselves. Words and language are important.

You should choose your words carefully. Use short sentences. Be clear and concise. Pick words that the audience understands and identifies with. Never, never use profanity or slang expressions. Here are some additional points to keep in mind regarding your choice of words.

- Do not use acronyms or other coded words unless you're absolutely sure that every person in the audience understands them.
- Do not use "bridge" words between sentences, such as "and," "also," "and another reason," etc. The problem here is overuse of the same word or group of words.
- Avoid the use of words that are highly popular at the time, unless they fit your message. As of this writing, *Yuppie* is popular, overused, and misused. Try to find more precise words for description.
- If you want to use a word that may not be understood by everyone in the audience, take the time to explain it.
- Watch your pet words and phrases. They may creep into your talk more often than you realize.
- Be most selective about the first sentence or two of your talk. Don't leave them to chance. Decide your exact words *before* you walk to the podium.
- Watch the gender. Use *salesperson* and not *salesman* (he versus she).
- Don't apologize for taking the audience's time, forgetting what you wanted to say, etc. Always remember that the audience is the recipient of your ideas and information; if anyone should apologize for anything, it would be the audience (for not listening, for example).
- Watch the use of the word *I*, especially when you're describing an accomplishment or in some way tooting your own horn. It

sounds a whole lot better to say, "We made our quota last year" than to say, "I made my quota."
- Be careful with the use of complex charts or graphs. Many salespeople will simply not understand them. Instead of showing a chart with two or three axes, show several charts, each with less complex information. Numbers can be frightening. Instead of saying that 32.75 percent of consumers preferred sample product A over sample product B, say instead, "We're keeping our old reliable *Gooey Crunchies* on the shelves because two out of three people liked them better than our new product!"
- Use comparisons to gain understanding. Say, "Our new high-speed packaging equipment turns out fifty twelve-ounce boxes of corn flakes every minute, which in a twenty-four-hour period will fill fourteen boxcars." If you want to bring the point home even further, you could then say, "Before I came here today, I determined how many boxcars of twelve-ounce corn flakes we now sell in this country on an average day. I hate to tell you this, but we're selling only eight boxcars per day. When I subtract eight from fourteen, I get six. It looks as though our work is cut out for us!"

Visual aids It takes a compelling speaker these days to hold audience interest for very long without the help of visual aids. Make your speaking chore a lot easier and your audience happier by utilizing a few props. These can be flip charts, chalkboards, hand-lettered posterboard, overhead transparencies, slides, film, videotape, and the like.

Visual aids need not be expensive. Use whatever material you have available. It's true that preparing props takes time, but the payoff is substantial. You will receive greater interest and attention from your audience, increase the recall of your speech, and improve understanding.

Tips on design Here are some tips on designing your visual aids.
1. Keep them simple.

2. Use key words only.

3. Make them clear and easily read from anywhere in the room.

4. Choose colors easily distinguished. Black or dark blue colors on a white background are easy to see. Red and pastel colors are difficult to read.

5. Avoid too much cleverness or cuteness in your design. It may detract from your main message.

6. Avoid the continued-on-the-next-slide syndrome. Never carry a sentence over to the next panel; restrict the number of panels on a single topic to about 20 (the fewer the better).

Tips on use

1. Don't keep a visual before the audience for more than a few minutes. When you're finished with a visual, put it away or cover it in some way. It can be distracting to the audience.

2. Use transparency frames to aid handling and also for making notes to yourself.

3. Don't darken the room any more than is necessary.

4. Don't look at the visuals, unless you're pointing something out. Look at the audience.

5. You may need to raise your voice slightly when using visuals, particularly if your slide projector or other equipment tends to be a bit noisy.

6. Use a pointer on the overhead transparency, not on the screen.

7. Turn equipment off as soon as you're finished with its use.

8. Have all equipment set up before you speak and test it, so that everything will run smoothly.

9. A screen can best be read when it's at a slight angle to the audience. Some speakers place the screen at the left or right side of the stage, slightly canted. In this way, their body and the projector itself will not block the audience's view of the screen.

10. Place the projector high enough so that you're not shooting upward toward the screen. This will avoid the keystone effect, which results in a somewhat distorted image.

©Dartnell Corporation

How to introduce a speaker

Always be brief. Tell the audience the speaker's name (say it slowly), title, and the organization he or she represents. Explain why the speaker is qualified to speak on the topic.

Any additional information may be interesting, but is not necessary. You could say that, "Old Joe, our company's research chemist, leads a boy scout troop and built a boat in his basement which was too large to get out," but what the audience really wants to hear is what Old Joe has to say about the formulation of that new floor wax, and what's in it that keeps the kitchen floor looking like new for 17 years!

Your last sentence should always repeat the speaker's name. When your introduction is finished, step aside and look in the direction of the approaching speaker. When the speaker arrives at his or her spot, wait briefly to see that the speaker has no problems and then move quickly away.

It's a good idea, especially if you're the master of ceremonies, to sit somewhere close to the speaker, so you'll be ready to jump up and reclaim the meeting leadership quickly, once the speaker has concluded. Never leave the room after introducing a speaker.

Some introducers feel that they should not state the speaker's name until the final sentence. This seems to be without foundation, unless the speaker is really supposed to be a surprise and is hiding just off stage. Most of your salespeople will know who's coming on next, so there's no reason to keep it a secret. Finally, remember to put a little enthusiasm in your introduction. How do you expect the troops to be interested and enthusiastic if you're not?

When the speaker has finished, say, "Thank you, Mr. ____ or Ms. ____, for sharing your thoughts (ideas, plans, etc.) with us today." Never, never summarize what the speaker said. That's his or her job. Don't try to tag on to what the speaker said or make implications that the speaker may or may not agree with. When a speech is over, it's over. Go on to the next topic or speaker as quickly as possible.

©Dartnell Corporation

Handling questions

Anticipate questions and be prepared to answer as briefly and as specifically as possible. Tell your audience at the beginning that you will take questions. Also tell them whether you will take questions during your talk and/or immediately afterwards.

If it's a large group and if amplification is needed for everyone to hear the questions, always repeat the question before answering it.

If you're not sure the questioner understood your answer, ask him or her to explain your reply.

If you anticipate far more questions than time in which to answer, give each member of the audience one or more 3 x 5 cards, instructing them to write one question on each card. Collect the cards immediately after you finish your talk. Read each one quickly, put the duplicates together, and then select and put in priority order the questions as you want to answer them. This will allow time for the most important questions (in your judgment) as well as those that were asked by more than one person.

Getting the questioning started is sometimes a problem. This can be solved by planting one or two questions among the audience prior to the start of your speech.

Two handy forms for use in developing your presentations are shown in Figures 1 and 2 on pages 185 and 186.

©Dartnell Corporation

**Figure 1.
Presentation
Plan
Worksheet**

Presentation topic _____
Time, date, place _____
Who requested? _____
Objectives _____
_____
_____
_____
_____

Who are they? Attitudes, knowledge of topic _____
_____
_____
_____
_____

Main points _____
_____
_____
_____
_____

©Dartnell Corporation

Figure 2. Presentation Worksheet

Topic _____

Who's doing it? _____

Date, time, place _____

How many expected? _____

How will room be arranged? _____
_____

What aids will be needed? _____
_____
_____

Who's in charge of aids? _____
_____

Handouts _____
_____

How distributed? _____
_____

Experts needed _____
_____

©Dartnell Corporation

Section 18

Arranging for Transportation

Getting there may be half the fun, although maybe not these days, considering the vagaries of air transportation since deregulation of the airline industry in 1978. Regardless of horror stories of lost luggage, missed connections, and late arrivals and departures, air travel remains the cheapest and most efficient method of getting from one place to another, including getting to sales meetings.

Centralizing the location to provide maximum convenience (and the lowest possible cost) for all involved is, of course, the key to planning transportation. The factor of time enters into the equation, too. The speedy pace of business these days doesn't allow for the leisurely travel of even ten or 20 years ago. Increasingly, time is money.

Getting to the meeting

Once you have decided on the location of your meeting (see Section 14), your next consideration should be how your people are going to get there and who will pay for the trip. In most cases your people will arrive and depart via commercial airlines, which is all the more reason that your site selection process should be carefully thought out. Oddly enough, it is not at all easy to get to some locations in this country highly touted as "the perfect location for your meeting." True, these so-called perfect locations may well have ample amenities for the meeting, but if more than one form of transportation is required, these location advantages (even room prices) dissipate rapidly.

Hub city advantages

One of the results of deregulation is the fact many medium to small cities are difficult to reach without changes of flights or carriers. Therefore, it behooves you to situate your meeting in or near the places that the airline industry has chosen as hub cities. Some of the

©Dartnell Corporation

major hubs are Atlanta, Memphis, Denver, New York, Newark, and Minneapolis. There are numerous others, depending on the carrier involved.

Locating your meeting in or near an airline hub solves one of your major transportation problems immediately: chances are good that your salespeople will arrive—with their luggage—fairly close to scheduled time and ready to get down to business. Also, flights to hubs, or between them, frequently are discounted when reservations are made far enough in advance (another good reason to pick your site early and advise everyone of all meeting logistics as far in advance as possible).

Hub cities also have another advantage for the meeting planner: they are equipped for almost any kind of meeting; some even have major meeting hotels and convention centers virtually within walking distance of the terminal. These sites, too, generally provide another major service to the meeting planner: they have frequent airport pick-up service to and from the hotel, sometimes at no cost to the traveler. Considering taxi services in most cities nowadays, this a major advantage, particularly to someone not familiar with the airport of the city.

Who pays? The major question to be resolved in meeting transportation has to do with your budget for the session. In essence, who is going to pay the transportation tab? The individual salesperson? the firm? or will costs be split? The answer to this question depends on the individual firm and corporate policies.

The company The recent trend is for the company to pick up the basic tab, i.e., the round-trip coach fares from city of origin. A potential disadvantage is that the individual salesperson—if allowed to make his or her own reservations—may not pay much attention to early reservation discounts if he or she is not paying. Such discounts can be sizable. The best technique, and one not difficult to handle if you do steady business with a reputable travel agent, is to turn over the reservations problem to the travel agent. Keep in mind that your travel agent must be a savvy type and, most of all, have computer hook-ups in his or her office to constantly keep tabs on changing airline fares. During peak seasons airline fares often change overnight, depending mostly on competitive factors within the industry.

If it is your decision (one we recommend) to pay the freight to and from the meeting, Figure 1, below, shows a suggested form to use for each person coming to the meeting by air. One form for each person will greatly simplify the work of your travel agency and also will serve as a record for you of flights, reservations, and cost. Get these forms (one for each salesperson) to your travel agent at least six weeks prior to the meeting (preferably earlier) and stress that you are interested in all discounts available. The latter is entirely possible these days, particularly if you have volume business on one airline, because of competitive practices within the industry. When you

Figure 1. Airline Reservation Form

```
Salesperson_____
                          (Full Name)
Address_____
Telephone_____    _____
              (Home)                        (Office)
From_____ To_____
       (Departure point)              (Destination)
Round trip?_____ Carrier(s)_____
Cost_____        Discount_____
Flight dates_____ _____
              (En route)                (Return)
Departure times  _____  _____  Arrivals  _____  _____
                (En route) (Return)          (En route) (Return)
Return this form when filled in to _____
                                        (Your name)
_____  _____  _____
      (Firm name)              (Address)            (Phone)
with appropriate ticket attached.

                              _____
                                   (Signature)
                              _____
                                     (Date)
```

©Dartnell Corporation

receive these forms back, with tickets attached, forward each individually to the salesperson involved. You will then have a record of when each person is due to arrive.

The airline itself is an excellent resource to help you figure out the transportation to and from the meeting. All airlines have people specifically charged with handling travel arrangements. For instance, if you can get ten people together, all leaving from the same destination, you have what most airlines call a group. Such a group qualifies for a discount, which can be as high as 30 percent. Thus, if you have a concentration of ten salespeople in, say, the New York area, and your convention is going to be in Chicago, it pays to book all the New York metropolitan reps on the same flight out. Going home, they can be on their own—just as long as they stay on the same airline both ways.

Airlines base flight charges on traffic demands, meaning that it usually pays to include a Saturday in your meeting plans. Airlines also offer a number of other services to people traveling in groups. You must ask; don't expect them to volunteer special services or pricing. Most airlines, if your account seems valuable, will agree to allow the use of VIP lounges for groups. This may not be important in itself, but it can be an ego boost to the sales representatives.

Among other advantages to group travel to sales meetings are such things as in-flight imprinted menus, various giveaways (such as sightseeing guides, baggage tags, and restaurant guides), and special luggage handling, where a group's luggage is bunched together and placed on the plane last for speedy identification at the terminal. The thing to keep in mind is that the backbone of the airline business is and will remain the business traveler. Thus, most airlines are not only equipped to offer special services to a group but are eager to do so.

The salespeople If it is not the policy of your firm to pay for the transportation of sales reps to meetings, there's still a lot you can do to assist in the process. You can arrange for the previously discussed group rates and make reservations through the firm's travel agency. The only difference in the procedures already outlined is that the sales rep must reimburse the firm for his or her transportation. Regardless, the operative thought here should be that there's discount in numbers, and few sales reps will quarrel with the idea of saving on his or her transportation bill to the meeting.

Keep in mind, too, that if for some reason you select a site that is blatantly inconvenient to many of your personnel, you will not only hear about it, but color the tone of the meeting even before it starts. Site location is the key to the question of transportation, no matter who is paying.

Getting things organized in advance for the meeting is crucial. Telling everyone in advance where the meeting is going to be (assuming your people pay their way to and from) allows for a variety of travel options, down to and including car-pooling if the distance is not too great. If the firm does not pick up the bill on accommodations at the meeting, your people should know meeting dates and locations far enough in advance to have a choice in optional housing. For example, Salesman X very well may have close relatives or friends in the convention city and would prefer to stay with them during the off-time. However, relatives and friends, close as they may be, need some notice.

If it is policy for the salespeople to pay for transportation and housing at the meeting, investigate ways in which they can save money. Is a cab ride from the airport to the hotel exorbitant? Does the hotel have a shuttle bus to and from the airport? If so, where does it pick up? These details, which you should get from the hotel or convention center, should be passed on to the sales force as soon as you are aware of them.

If spouses are coming along, it is essential to outline all the wonders of the city in which the meeting is being held, including shopping, concerts, theater, museums, and nightlife. These considerations, while they may seem minor in the total picture, will help to create an atmosphere of cooperation at the meeting itself. All of these factors apply, too, in a shared expense situation in which costs are split between the firm and the salesperson.

©Dartnell Corporation

Ground transportation

Not infrequently, your transportation worries don't end with just getting things organized in the air. You also have to think of ground transportation, which can include anything from travel to and from the airport to bus tours of company facilities.

If you are using a major hub city convention or meeting location, such as a chain hotel, you'll likely find that the hotel maintains a steady shuttle bus service to and from the airport. This is not only for business travelers but also for the casual tourist. If the hotel you have chosen does not provide such service, it pays to look into public transportation to and from the airport. Many major cities have concentrated on fast and inexpensive public transportation between downtown and the airport but, in the maze of most modern airports, finding such services can become a career. Thus, investigate public transportation services from the airport and pinpoint where they can be found.

Check out car rental facilities and prices at the airport. Car rentals can vary as widely as airline ticket prices. Some of the most reasonable car rentals can be obtained a few miles from the airport, at locations you can reach by shuttle bus service. It pays to shop around in arranging for rental cars where group discounts apply. Advance reservations are necessary with almost any car rental agency, so this form of ground transportation must be nailed down in advance.

The point of doing this advance legwork becomes apparent when you consider how much time you have spent in airports looking for the shuttle buses of a particular car rental agency.

Have car rental information in the hands of the salespeople before they get off their incoming planes. They'll not only thank you, but you will later be dealing with a more receptive audience.

If your meeting calls for bus trips, either to visit plant facilities or new headquarters under construction, book your transportation as far in advance as possible, and make sure you know the costs involved in running over your allotted time for using the bus. These costs can be a grim surprise if not monitored closely. Typically, a charter bus capable of seating 45 will cost you about $45 to $50 for four hours, with overtime averaging around $20 an hour.

Book early and, if possible, book through your hotel. Most major meeting hotels have arrangements with some carriers, meaning that the drivers know the ins and outs of the hotel and are allowed certain proximity privileges in loading and unloading not accorded other lines.

Section 19

Getting Meeting Rooms Ready

Now we come to the part of this manual that separates the professionals from the amateurs—setting up the room or rooms. Check your room at least an hour before your meeting is scheduled to begin. Sounds simple, doesn't it? It's not, usually. It is not necessary to catalog all the disasters that have been known to occur to sabotage your scrupulously planned meeting at this point, but some include change of meeting room, power outages, missing audio-visual equipment, flood, fires, etc.

This is the time when you find out who your friends are. Despite all the planning you have gone through, chances are good that something will go wrong with the physical set-up in the meeting room. Maybe the hotel staff goofed. Maybe there aren't enough chairs. Maybe the air conditioning isn't working. Any number of last-minute emergencies can and do arise.

Your meeting is still salvageable. If the hotel has changed your room, be sure that they have also changed the meeting board and that there are notices posted at the original room redirecting your attendees. Station someone to round-up and direct stragglers. This individual should be easily identifiable as a member of your group. In this way, the start of your meeting should be delayed only a few minutes. Focus on running the meeting, rather than on the hotel's mistake. You can vent your anger later.

The best you can do is be prepared. By that we mean, have a cadre of associates and friends on the sales force who are not averse to using some brawn if required.

©Dartnell Corporation

Setting up the meeting room breaks down into two major categories of detail: equipment necessary for the session in place and the physical set-up of the room.

Let's tackle the physical layout first.

Physical layout

Auditorium or theater style

Excellent for large groups of up to 400, the auditorium, or theater, style is generally the easiest set-up, since chairs normally are fixed in place. Therefore, you don't have to be concerned about such things as local fire regulations or distances between rows. Along with a podium and a mike, there will normally be a small table up front for speakers. Be sure to provide a pitcher of ice water on that table, as well as at several locations along the walls for participants.

If the seating is not permanent, be sure to have seats placed at least two inches apart and allow 33 inches between rows, or more if you have the room. Cramped quarters not only are frowned on by most local fire ordinances, but prove annoying and distracting. Allow a center aisle at least six feet wide, and break up the group with side aisles at about every 15 chairs.

Sample auditorium set-ups are shown in Figure 1, page 197.

Tablet armchairs if available

These commendable pieces of furniture are a fine bet. Tablet armchairs provide room for note taking—usually important at any meeting—such as in discussions of new and complex sales policies or commission structures. Keep these chairs at least three inches apart, with distance between chair rows at least 36 inches, center to center.

Meeting set-ups at tables

These set-ups are by far the most commonly used in smaller sales meetings and they can take a variety of forms, depending on the size of your group, how well members of the group know one another, and the formality factor of the meeting itself. Whatever arrangement you choose, all tables should be neatly covered with clean, ironed tablecloths. The most popular set-up arrangements are the following:

Conference. This is nothing more than a conference table, usually rectangular (See Figure 2, page 199), with the meeting leader at the head of the table and the other participants seated along the sides and at the foot. If the group is small—up to 20—the conference

Getting Meeting Rooms Ready 197

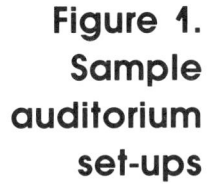

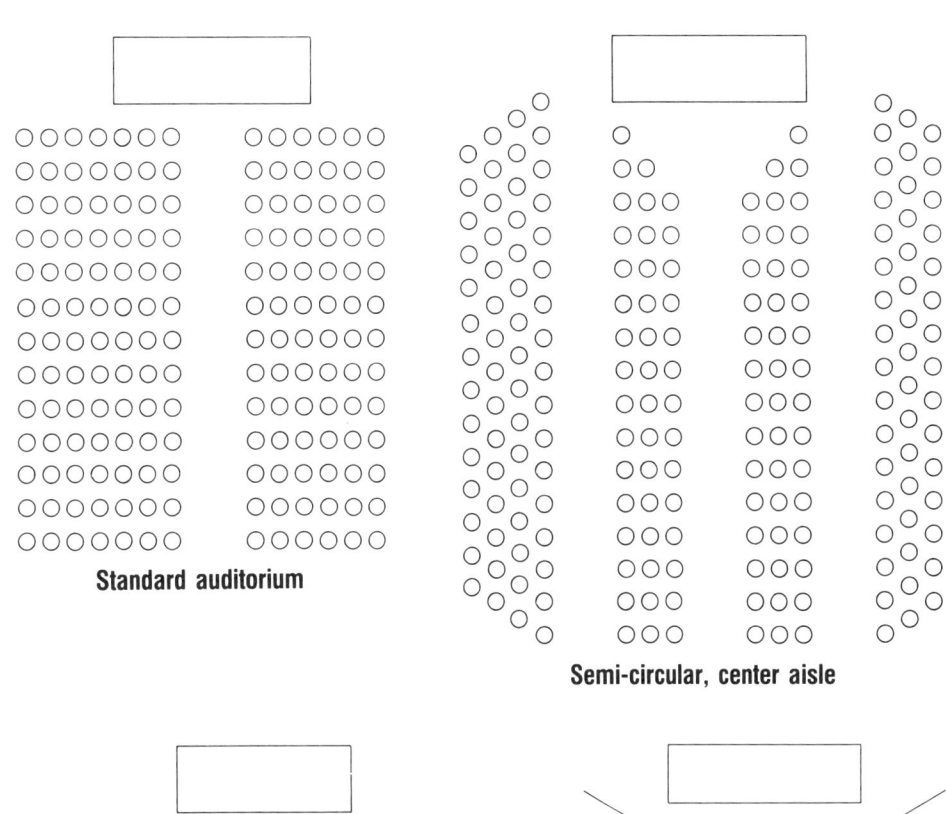

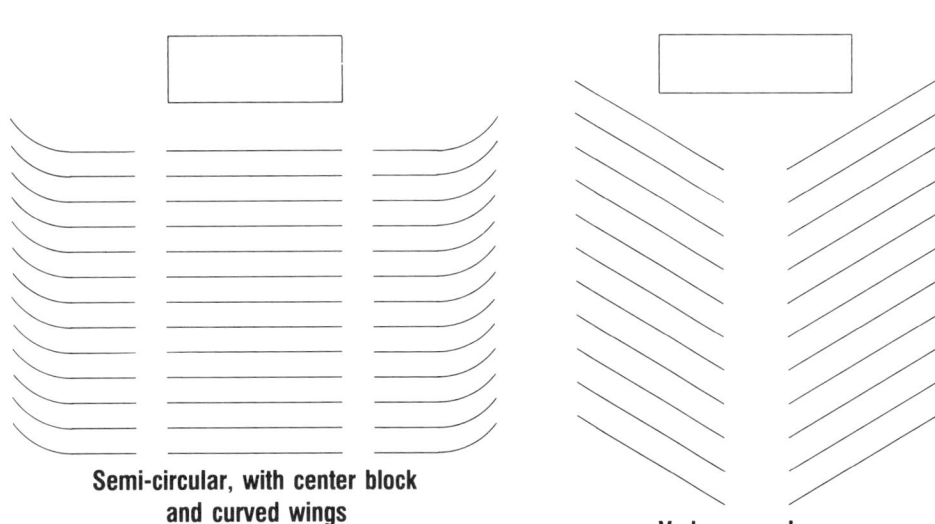

Figure 1. Sample auditorium set-ups

Standard auditorium

Semi-circular, center aisle

Semi-circular, with center block and curved wings

V-shape or chevron

©Dartnell Corporation

set-up usually works very well. It's a sort of shirt-sleeve, let's-level-with-each-other atmosphere.

U-shaped. This arrangement is set up with a combination of rectangular tables (See Figure 3, page 199), with size of the table dependent on attendance you anticipate. Usually, at least 24 inches of table space per person is necessary. If your people require a lot of papers for the meeting (price manuals, new forms, etc.), allow more space for each individual. As with other table set-ups, pencils and pads should be provided for each space. Tables should be about 18 inches wide and 6 to 8 feet long. Generally, seat three people at a 6-foot table and 4 people at an 8-foot one. Chairs should be set about a foot away from the table. The U-shape is a desirable set-up when the group is somewhat larger than 20, or when a conference set-up would be impossible because of the number of people to be seated.

E-shaped. This is the same idea as the U-shaped arrangement, except that an extra seating arm extends from the head table between the two outer arms (See Figure 4, page 199). Care should be taken here to allow plenty of room (at least four feet) between the backs of chairs inside the E legs to allow easy access to seating. While the E-shape is used frequently with medium-size groups (50 or so), it has the disadvantage of cutting off sight lines for those seated far down the outer legs of the E.

T-shaped. This can best be accomplished by setting up a six-foot by 30-inch table as the head table and then extending from this table a double-width (60-inch) table as long as is needed for the people you expect (See Figure 5, page 199). This arrangement serves admirably in place of the U-shape. Again, allow at least 24 inches of table space per person.

Hollow square. This is a similar set-up to the U-shape, except that the open end of the U is filled with a table(s) (See Figure 6, page 199). Chairs are placed on the outside only.

Round tables. This amounts, almost, to the same thing as the conference set-up (See Figure 7, page 199). The main difference—and sometimes a decided advantage—is that the round table set-up is more conducive to eye contact than any other arrangement. This

Getting Meeting Rooms Ready 199

Figures 2-7.

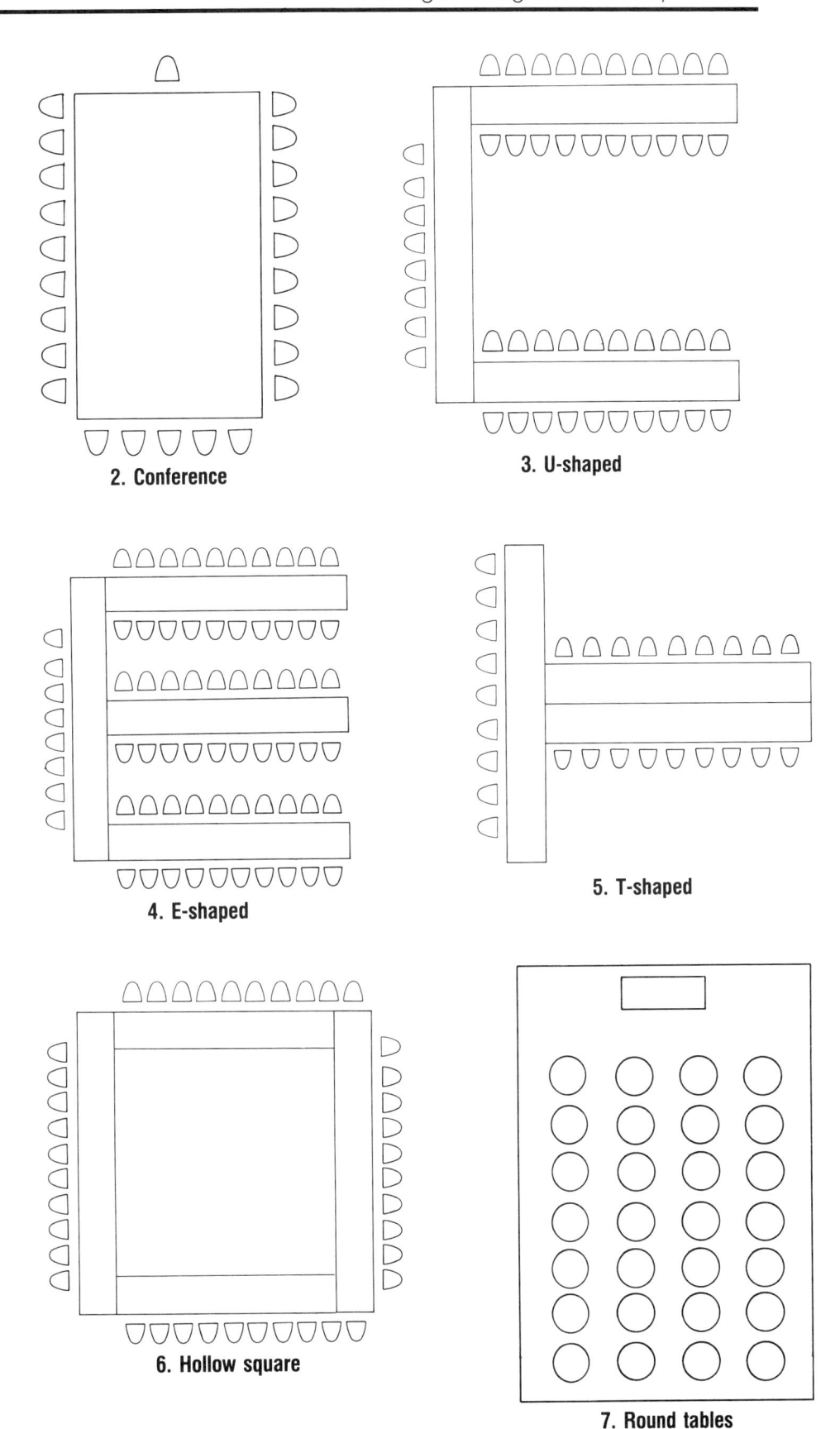

2. Conference

3. U-shaped

4. E-shaped

5. T-shaped

6. Hollow square

7. Round tables

©Dartnell Corporation

allows for greater informality and, frequently, greater frankness in expression. Basically, what it amounts to is that you can observe a person's facial expressions (as well as voice) as he or she talks. Round tables also can be used in an auditorium meeting set-up, with five or so people grouped at each table. This has the advantage of allowing for easy team work during the course of the meeting. This set-up also allows for a less stodgy atmosphere within a large group—the group within a group concept. In some circumstances, particularly when workshop sessions will be involved, this is a great advantage.

Schoolroom style. This arrangement is just what the name implies—a speaker's table in front center, with tables for the audience lined up along the center aisle to the rear of the room. The advantage this traditional arrangement provides is generally good sight lines for all participants, particularly if the speaker's table is elevated. The disadvantage is that the arrangement speaks of formality, which can inhibit participation.

The schoolroom arrangement comes in several variations, including the V-shape, or chevron, and the perpendicular arrangement of tables for participants. All these variations are illustrated in Figure 8, page 201.

Lighting In getting the meeting room ready, it is important to do a dry run early in the day of the meeting to check on two critical factors: lighting and ventilation.

While most meeting locations come well equipped, don't leave anything to chance when it comes to lighting. First, do the overheads work? Do all bulbs work? Can the lights be controlled from a convenient switch near the speaker's table? Next, are there enough floor and wall outlets to handle the equipment you may wish to use during the meeting? Do the outlets work? Test all outlets you intend to use *before* trying to turn on the projector at the meeting. Nothing is more distracting during a meeting than a long pause while someone attempts to solve an electrical problem. Fixing the problem, after the meeting has started, can be a time-consuming affair in a strange environment.

Figure 8. Schoolroom arrangements

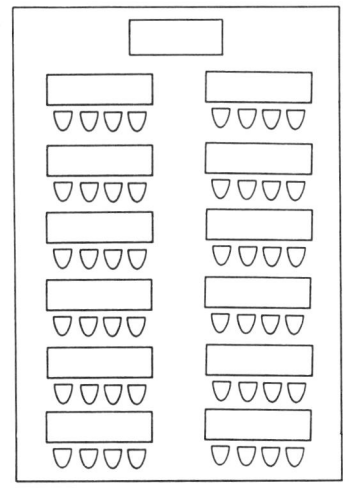

Basic schoolroom

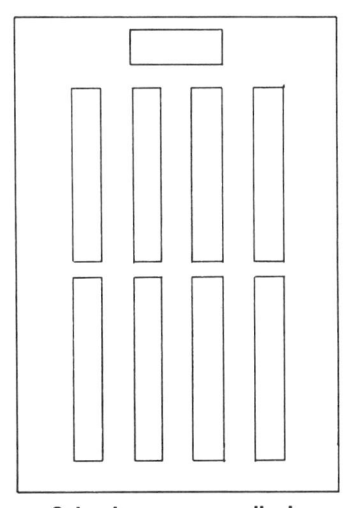

Schoolroom perpendicular

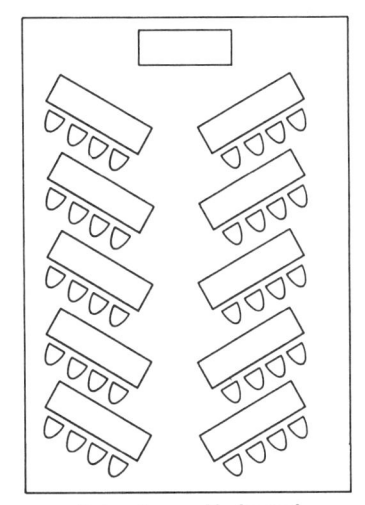

Schoolroom V-shaped

©Dartnell Corporation

Never rely on the hotel staff's assurances that all systems are go when setting up your meeting room. Make certain, too, that the voltages required at certain outlets are available through that outlet. Checking the lighting should be one of the last things you do right before the meeting.

Ventilation
You also should check the ventilation of the meeting room. Is there enough air movement? Is the thermostat working? Remember, too, that the ideal temperature for a meeting room is about 68 to 70°F; but with a lot of people in the room, an original setting of 68 degrees will not be sufficient to maintain the optimum temperature. Thus, it is a good idea to have the room initially cooler than comfortable. The temperature in a room full of people will rise rapidly.

Ventilation is all important, requiring a steady exchange of air to assure constant fresh air. Most meeting rooms these days are cooled, heated, and ventilated by a central system that serves the entire hotel, or most of the public rooms. It may be necessary to speak to a hotel executive about your room temperature requirements during negotiations. Then check when you arrive to see that your instructions have been carried out.

Good ventilation has become even more of a factor in audience comfort these days due to the controversy over smoking.

Are you going to ban smoking altogether in the meeting room? If so, you have no problem except, perhaps, lingering resentment on the part of the smokers.

If you do not ban smoking during the meetings, then you must consider the feelings of those opposed to breathing borrowed smoke—and the number of these people is on the rise. What's the solution?

The best solution—and it's not much of one, admittedly—is to create a smoking section within the meeting room, as close as possible to the air outlet duct and, preferably, at the rear of the room. If your group is small, and everyone knows one another, a smoking section may not be necessary. If your group is large, you should be alert to the possibility, particularly in large groups, that you face

©Dartnell Corporation

trouble right off the bat by mixing smokers with non-smokers in confined quarters.

Equipment

The next consideration is an equipment check. Do this immediately before the meeting. This last-minute inventory will save you a lot of hassling later when, for example, you discover that two of the product films are upstairs in your room. It's a good idea, in fact, to have a checklist of all equipment you need and, just after checking the lighting and ventilation in the room, to go over your checklist, a sample of which appears in Figure 9, below.

Most importantly, the person running the meeting needs to know exactly where every piece of equipment is. This can include such items as lecterns, platforms, blackboards, chalk, erasers, easels, projectors, projector tables, and pointers. If you are making new product introductions, check to see that the correct samples are all there and in order of presentation. It is essential that all these materials be at your immediate beck and call to avoid the long pauses you create by searching around, say, for an eraser or a piece of chalk.

Because nearly all meeting rooms have a certain amount of off-meeting traffic (cleaning crews, etc.), your equipment check must be conducted as near deadline as possible. Don't expect to have everything in the room in the same shape as you left it last night.

Figure 9. Meeting Room Equipment Checklist

In place	Checked by
Microphones_____	_____
Sound_____	_____
Projector_____	_____
Films_____	_____
Blackboard_____	_____
Lights, outlets_____	_____
Erasers, chalk_____	_____
Pads, pencils_____	_____
Remotes working_____	_____
Hotel contact_____	Ext. #_____

©Dartnell Corporation

Have you provided the sales staff with the various materials they will need in order to participate in the meeting? This includes pencils and paper at each setting, repros of a forthcoming ad campaign, etc. Do you have a reserve supply of basic materials, such as pencils and paper, at hand?

If you have arranged with a local supplier to provide audio-visual equipment, make sure you conduct a dry run with the sales rep on how the equipment operates. This is all-important. Technology in the audio-visual field is changing at an alarming rate and is not necessarily getting any simpler with its various advances. Make sure you know how to operate every piece of equipment you intend to use and that the rented equipment is compatible with your tapes or film.

Silly as it may sound, it even pays to practice putting the screen you intend to use up and down. How many times have you waited while someone struggled to unfold a screen and get it in place?

If you are fortunate enough to be hiring a projectionist, make sure he or she has a timed schedule of when he or she is needed.

Another tip: If you are not a genius when it comes to the care and feeding of a lot of the new whiz-bang audio-video equipment available, make it clear to the supplier from the outset that you want the simplest possible equipment and not necessarily the latest gadget he may wish to try out on you. You may get a good laugh by stumbling through a presentation involving the latest in audio-video, but will you get your primary message across? Keep it as simple as possible. Don't use this occasion to indulge your curiosity about what's new on the electronic media front.

©Dartnell Corporation

Section 20

Handling Food/Banquet Functions

Not too long ago—20 years or so—the food service function at a sales meeting was a fairly standardized procedure. You contacted the hotel official known as the banquet manager and outlined the number of meals needed, times, and places. You also provided a cost figure, the total, and then left the rest up to him (not many banquet managers 20 years ago were women).

That, of course, was before the word *nouvelle* came into the lexicon of food. That one simple French word meaning *new* did a lot to complicate the life of the sales meeting planner. The word is pervasive in commercial food establishments these days and is a red signal to meeting planners to plan and control the meal functions of their meetings with as much care as the planning of the agenda. Avoid extra-fancy food and the higher prices that usually go with it.

If you leave the food functions up to a hotel banquet manager's discretion these days, you risk rumbling revolution in the ranks or, worse, people ducking out to the nearest McDonald's for lunch. And who can blame them. Most salespeople want food they can recognize, especially after they've tasted it! Thus, the food functions at any meeting, large or small, must be planned to the last detail, with all your expectations outlined clearly. This means more work for the planner.

Your first consideration is the evaluation of the personal traits of your group. Are they old-shoe types? Are they young would-be sophisticates, or yuppies? Are they mainly from small towns and communities or from major cities?

This evaluation generally is easier than you may think. People of like backgrounds tend to have common interests and tastes—and

©Dartnell Corporation

gravitate to similar professions. They also, very likely, tend to have similar tastes in food and entertainment.

Because it is critical to get a handle on the food functions for your meeting early, it is a good idea to keep a progress report on file, as negotiations proceed with hotel personnel. A handy checklist and form such as the one shown in Figure 1, below, can prove useful.

Your first consideration in food function planning is to break down the number and types of meals involved. Will you have everybody on his or her own for breakfast? If the meeting site has ample coffee shop facilities (and if you are not planning a breakfast session), it is a good idea to let everyone take care of his or her own breakfast needs. For one thing, this saves time; for another, tastes in breakfasts are immensely varied. The old scrambled eggs, toast, and bacon menu is not agreeable to many people these days.

The coffee (soda) breaks are easier to handle, but, here again, there is an increasing number of people these days who eschew

Figure 1. Food Function Planner

Date_____

Meal	# Guests	Room - floor #	Time	Cost
Breakfast				
Breaks				
Lunch				
Reception				
Dinner				

Special meal requests_____
_____
_____

©Dartnell Corporation

coffee, even the decaf variety. Make sure you include tea, soda, and low calorie milk in your coffee break plans. Stress that you want break service ready on time and provide a muffin or pastry at the morning break for those who missed breakfast. Incidentally, it's a real kindness to provide coffee prior to the meeting, as well.

The luncheon buffet

Luncheon menus also can be tricky, with so many people concentrating on diets. This time of day, particularly if you have a long and important afternoon session scheduled, is not the time to serve a big, heavy meal. It also is not the time to promote the pre-lunch cocktail. It is, in fact, the appropriate time to schedule a buffet (if your group is large enough), making sure this includes a satisfactory salad bar.

Buffets, of course, come in all shapes and sizes, ranging from fairly reasonable to elaborately expensive. Keep your own people's tastes in mind.

An attractive (key to a good buffet) spread can be put together without getting too elaborate or excessive. Make this point clear to the banquet manager. In your discussions, you'll find that buffets generally are priced per head, taking into consideration the number of extras you require, such as ice sculptures, etc. If the hotel serves its own buffet in the public rooms, try to check out the quality and quantity of the presentation and scale down your own buffet from the one available to the general public.

Another advantage of the buffet, particularly for lunch, is that it is a time-saver. Because fewer employees are needed by the hotel to serve a buffet, the cost per meal will likely be lower. Most up-to-date hotels can set up, serve, and remove a buffet in much less time than it takes for a sit-down, served meal.

The banquet

The banquet, as noted earlier, has come a long way in 20 or so years, and not just because of the influence of nouvelle cuisine on the current crop of hotel chefs!

Gone (some things do change for the better) are the tepid and oleaginous offerings that once were standard fare on banquet menus.

You'd probably search a long time these days to find creamed chicken on a banquet menu. Now banquets usually offer the individual diner a choice of entree, with fish usually included as a choice, and with rice a substitute for potatoes. Here again, if the hotel does not offer a choice, which seems unlikely, insist on either a chicken or fish alternative to the roast beef or ham. Insist, too, on a choice of desserts, with at least one light (low calorie) offering.

You should establish how the banquet is going to be served: so-called French service, where the food is placed individually on the plates of each diner; Russian service, where diners help themselves to food passed around by waiters; or plate service, where entrees are brought from the kitchen completely assembled. The last is by far the most efficient form of service and the one most used by major hotels.

It is also important to remember that at least two feet of space should be allowed for each diner. Do not allow the hotel to crowd people elbow to elbow for a banquet or any other food function.

If the banquet involves a program, and they normally do, outline in advance the facilities you will need and how many people should be seated at the head table. Usually hotel personnel are skilled at meeting your needs in this department, but they can't read your mind. All audio-visual equipment should be checked out before people sit down for the banquet.

Most hotels which cater to the meeting/convention trade have good service and preparation down to an almost exact science, and their banquet managers will be well equipped to assist in menu planning, as well as to offer clues to the chef's specific talents or enthusiasms. Generally these suggestions take the form of specific menus within specific price categories, with pricing frequently dependent on the seasonal nature of the hotel traffic. Sometimes there are remarkable bargains to be found, simply because traffic is slow at the hotel and the permanent staff needs to be kept occupied. Hotels won't as a rule volunteer such information, but contacts in convention bureaus will. Determine the on-off seasons at the location you select before entering into negotiations on menu planning.

©Dartnell Corporation

Planning the menu

No one says a meeting planner must be a qualified nutritionist, but it helps if you know something about current and popular nutrition trends in planning your meeting's menus with the hotel. Here are a few tips.

- Make sure that at least one fish and one poultry alternative is available at each luncheon and banquet.
- Avoid selecting heavy entrees, particularly fried, greasy foods.
- Stress as many vegetables as possible (not, if possible, the steam table versions of same).
- Offer an assortment of beverages, diet sodas, decaf coffee and tea, and low calorie milk.
- Make sure sugar and salt substitutes are available on every table.
- Avoid any temptation to stray into exotic menu offerings.
- Offer a fruit and cheese choice for dessert.
- Offer a choice of salad dressing, including low calorie.

Assuming you have done business with the hotel before and know and trust the banquet manager and his or her staff, much of your preliminary work in handling the food functions will be taken care of for you. This is a distinct advantage in terms of time and worry saved.

However, the hotel and food service industry is afflicted these days with high turnover, and what was true at the same location last year may not apply at all this year. Thus it is best to get it all down in writing, even if you know and trust the manager. This is an advantage to him or her, too, because if misunderstandings do arise (and food service usually is the major source of contention at sales gatherings), you can settle the problem quickly by simply referring to your written mutual agreement.

Other planning considerations

Even if you don't know the food service manager from past experience, approach this person in a spirit of cooperation. His or her aim is to give you the best possible service (to lure repeat business) at a profit to the hotel. Excessive demands generally will get you nowhere, which is not to say that you shouldn't try for any and all extras you feel are available and which you might be entitled to. It's good to remember, too, that food service managers are highly professional (and harassed) these days. They have to be. Cost and profit margins are fine, meaning that there is virtually no room for error. You cannot, for example, expect the hotel to pick up after your mistakes in judging attendance at food functions. You must be as precise as possible about the number of people expected at each food and/or cocktail function. Hotels price by the person, and margins allow for little or no variation from the planned estimate. Be prepared to pick up the tab for meals prepared but not eaten, or for the extra plates served if you have underestimated your attendance.

Determine in your initial negotiations just how you will be charged for your food functions—a signed guarantee, collected tickets, or by quantity. Find out in advance what the cut-off date is for guaranteed numbers of meals or covers. It will be at least 48 hours in advance (some hotels require 72 hours notice). When discussing meal guarantees, inquire the percent over your guarantee that the hotel will prepare. You'll pay only for the number of meals guaranteed, or number served (whichever is greater), but it's reassuring to know that if a few additional folks show up, they will be fed.

It is your responsibility to know the number of people who will show up at any meal function. It is also your responsibility to assume the costs of incorrect projections.

The cut-off time on guaranteed attendance is a constant battle between meeting planners and hotel personnel. If you deem a 24-hour guarantee unreasonable, then perhaps you will have to simplify your menu.

The same approach works when you want the hotel to set places for more than the 5 to 10 percent above guarantee, which is usually offered. If you want a higher number of places set, consider accepting different food for latecomers or order a simpler menu with easily prepared entrees which can hold for the late arrivals.

Virtually every hotel or convention site will require a meal guarantee from you before signing a contract for services. This spells out for both parties the exact number expected for each meal function or cocktail party, along with the menu for each meal. There is little room for error, once this agreement has been signed.

A sample guarantee form and menu requirement is shown in Figure 2 on page 212. It is best to use something similar for your own files, even though you very well may have to sign similar forms provided by the facility.

Alcohol service

The subject of alcohol service deserves special consideration. Your meeting attendees will expect that there will be alcohol served at pre-dinner and dinner functions, but laws and attitudes about alcohol are changing rapidly, and you should be aware of potential pitfalls.

Hotels and restaurants report that alcohol consumption is way down, due both to increased interest in health and fitness, and because of tougher drunk driving laws.

It would be wise to check the law of the state in which you're holding your meeting. Seventeen states have liquor liability laws which extend to the social host. This means that if your company provides a self-service bar at a cocktail party or hospitality suite, or a company employee serves as bartender, the company is liable in the event of an alcohol-related incident. This includes the seemingly innocuous practice of providing self-service kegs of beer for a party or sporting event.

On the other hand, if the hotel provides the bartender, it assumes liability. It makes sense to let the hotel's insurance carrier take the risk, rather than the company for which you're planning the meeting.

It's a good idea to limit the cocktail function to a brief 45 minutes to an hour, making sure there is plenty of food available. If your cocktail function is to be followed by a dinner, it is perfectly acceptable to keep the food minimal, perhaps providing peanuts, chips, or a cheese tray. You must plan much heavier hors d'oeuvres if there is no dinner planned to follow. Hotels sell hors d'oeuvres by the piece. A tray may contain 50 pieces (enough to serve eight people, following the rule of 6 pieces per person per hour).

©Dartnell Corporation

Figure 2. Food Function Guarantee Form

Please sign and return to:

_____ _____
(Name)   (Phone)

_____
(Address)

Location_____
Meeting_____
Dates_____
Hotel_____
Hotel Phone ( ) _____
Contact_____ Ext._____

Services Required

Meals

  Breakfast

    Room_____ Date_____
    Time_____ (See attached menu)
    Number_____

  Luncheon

    Room_____ Date_____
    Time_____ (See attached menu)
    Number_____

  Dinner

    Room_____ Date_____
    Time_____ (See attached menu)
    Number_____

  Breaks

    Room_____ Date_____
    Time_____ (See attached menu)
      (A.M.)   (P.M.)
    Number_____

Copies to:

  Catering Mgr.   ☐
  Kitchen   ☐
  Meeting Mgr.   ☐

The above requirements are understood and will be provided.

Signed_____ Date_____

Position_____

Hotel Name_____ Location_____

©Dartnell Corporation

You should be aware that while total consumption of liquor has decreased markedly, wine, beer, and bottled water remain very popular. It is common sense to be sure that there are non-alcoholic alternatives readily available at any cocktail function. You may be surprised at the number of people who elect sparkling water!

Having said all that, if your company wants to plan a cocktail party, you should understand how the hotel bills for liquor. You will have to decide whether you want to contract liquor service by the drink or by the bottle. If by the bottle, you will pay for each bottle opened, even if only one drink was poured. The opened bottle is, however, the property of the company, and should be taken after the function is over.

A bottle of liquor will serve approximately 30 drinks. Depending on the size of your group, this may be the least expensive. The guideline here is 2 drinks per person per hour. You can limit the variety of choices. Be sure that the bartender knows who is authorized to order another bottle.

The alternative is liquor by the drink. The bar is stocked with a certain amount of liquor, with any additional bottles inventoried as they are added. There are several ways to handle payment. Often tickets are issued to attendees, which are good for 1 drink each; sometimes the company simply sets the time limit, and is liable for drinks served during that time. In this type of service, tax and tip are included in the price of each drink served, but the price of the bartender will be additional.

Someone should be with the hotel contact during the liquor inventory following this event, to make sure there is an agreement on how much is to be billed for liquor.

Figure 3 on page 214 shows a suggested checklist for your food and beverage functions which, while cut to the bone, offers some idea of how complex the planning of food functions can be for any meeting.

Figure 3. Menu Form

Date_____
(Use one form for each day)

Location_____
Meeting_____
Dates_____
Hotel_____
Hotel Phone ( ) _____
Contact_____ Ext._____

Menu

Breakfast   Cost (Tax & gratuity)

    Entree_____   _____

    Drink_____   _____

Lunch

    Soup/salad_____ _____

    Entree_____   _____

    Dessert_____   _____

    Drink_____   _____

Dinner

    Soup/salad_____ _____

    Entree_____   _____

    Dessert_____   _____

    Drink_____   _____

Copies to:

    Catering mgr.   ☐

    Kitchen   ☐

    Meeting mgr.   ☐

©Dartnell Corporation

Section 21

Managing the Entertainment

There comes a time in any meeting when the mood just has to be lightened and professional entertainment is called for. Usually, this time will be just after the banquet, the social highlight of the meeting.

Appropriate entertainment

Planning entertainment for your meeting can be a tricky procedure. You first have to consider what is appropriate for your particular group of salespeople and, sometimes, for their spouses. If your group is mainly family-oriented, you will be better off not to choose ribald stand-up comedians or lounge singers. If your audience will be mostly people 40 and under, be careful that the artists you select are up-to-date on the music and jokes that this generation understands and appreciates.

There is a type of entertainment for all people in this world. It is your judgment call to assess what type most of your people are and to select your entertainers accordingly. Tastes in music change from generation to generation, and what you think might be upbeat and fun for meeting entertainment very well may be a drag to most of your group. In sum, don't select your entertainment and entertainers from your own prejudice or perspective. Most particularly, do not select your entertainment from any rigid moral code to which you may subscribe. Ask yourself, Who are these people in the audience? What styles in music, comedy, and dance turn them on? You may find yourself agreeing that a rock band is appropriate. If it is, book it and use the experience to try to understand the younger set.

Solid professional entertainers are available in almost all major cities in the country today, thanks to the growth in regional theater

©Dartnell Corporation

and the ability of the young to pay for it. Gone are the days when the most some communities could offer in terms of professional entertainment was a pick-up band with a singer. In addition, most major hotels across the land have live entertainment in their lounges and bistros, at least on the weekends.

Inappropriate entertainment

While it's not all that difficult to figure out what is appropriate in terms of entertainment for your group, it is not as easy to figure out what's inappropriate. However, it is obviously inappropriate to book strippers or exotic dancers at most sales gatherings; nor is it appropriate, as an extreme example, to book "drag" shows for a sales convention, regardless of talented performers. Comedians who traffic in ethnic and "blue" material also are out of bounds, even though some of these comics can clean up their acts for the occasion.

If your audience classifies as young (40 or under), you're not likely to achieve much in the way of entertainment by booking singers or bands who perform Lawrence Welk material. Many of the regional rock bands can be suspect for sales meeting entertainment purposes, too, because of the lyrics they write and perform.

Before signing the performance contract, ask yourself if the act, singer, dancer, comedian, or ventriloquist is appropriate to the surroundings and tone of the group.

If you have questions about the appropriateness of an entertainer for your meeting, make sure you catch his or her act before committing yourself. If this is not possible, and if the performer is a singer, ask for a demo tape.

The size and layout of the room in which the artist will be performing is very important, as well. Some fine vocalists simply do not come across in any environment except a small, dimly-lit room. Some comics have an intimate style that breaks up audiences at midnight in a bistro, but leaves a larger audience cold.

Another consideration in planning entertainment for your meeting is how much time you will have with the entertainer(s) to explain what kind of program you prefer. Will the performer do a run-through? Short of that, will he or she explain the act briefly to you? Will he or she require a rehearsal with a band? Is the performer flexible (within limits) on time?

One of the most embarrassing things that can happen to a meeting planner is to book an act sight unseen only to discover during the performance that it is all wrong for the group. Or, worse yet, that the performer would be better off leaving show business.

In planning your entertainment, keep in mind the physical limitations of the performance areas and the lighting required. Most performers are expert at adjusting to almost any circumstance, but all require some sort of stage and a spotlight.

Most seasoned performers, big or small time, are more than eager to pick up spare change by playing conventions or sales meetings. Even some of the biggest names are available—if you book far enough in advance. The material they use for conventions, trade shows, and sales meetings generally is tried, true, and surefire. If the performer is at all well known, he or she is known for some specialty, which will be used in the act.

One of the cleverest acts ever to play the convention and sales meeting circuit was a zany guy named Professor Irwin Corey, who had a simple enough, but surefire act: doubletalk on some weighty subject. He made no sense at all but he took himself so seriously that what he didn't say was hilarious.

Hiring entertainment

Once you have decided what kind of entertainment you want (and consider appropriate), how do you go about arranging to hire it for the meeting? This is not as mysterious as it may seem at first glance. Remember that the operative word in the phrase *show business* is *business*.

There are a variety of methods of contacting and booking entertainment for your meetings. Among them are the following:

- Consult with your hotel contact. He or she very likely will be current on what acts will be in town during your meeting.
- Ask the local convention bureau contact for the names of reputable booking agents in the city where you plan the meeting. All major cities have theatrical booking agencies these

days, some of which specialize in entertainment for conventions, trade shows, and meetings.

- Contact the booking agent recommended and explain what you have in mind, how much you are willing to pay, and when you need the act. Keep in mind that the booking agent will get a percentage of the fee you are paying (usually 10 percent), so the fee quoted might be open to negotiation.

- If the convention is going to be near your headquarters, check out local live entertainment personally if you can, and make personal contact. In almost all cases, this will lead you to an agent who will handle the details of booking and draw up necessary contracts, which normally are not complicated. These contracts spell out terms of payment, price, and, sometimes, conditions of employment, such as dressing rooms, length of performance (minimum), and, in the case of really big names, various other amenities, such as limousine service, back-up bands, etc.

Those who hold their meetings in the larger cities such as New York, Los Angeles, and Chicago can draw from a huge and impressive pool of talent, but even major hotels in secondary cities (and some resort communities) frequently play host to touring acts that will be more than happy to pick up some fast money by playing your meeting.

When you settle money and time terms with the entertainer or his or her agent, make certain that you then nail down the requirements of the performer in terms of dressing rooms, lighting, and music. Generally this can be handled best by working with your hotel contact.

Section 22

Planning for Emergencies

By this time, if you've stayed with us, you've probably gotten the impression that putting on a sales meeting is a lot of work. Your impression is correct. It is not only a lot of work, but often a lot of worry. You can minimize the worry factor by planning for emergencies. Rest assured that there will be some, and the size of the meeting has very little to do with it. In fact, the bigger the meeting, the fewer the crises.

The reason a big meeting can be the most trouble-free is that big meetings normally are stage-managed by experienced people who do nothing else. If you are like most of us, and have to wear several hats within your firm (all of which demand daily attention), the likelihood of something going awry at the meeting is high. It's the time when Murphy's Law lurks just around the corner.

Avoiding pitfalls

To help you avoid some of the pitfalls inherent in any sales meeting, here are some proven suggestions.

1. Ask yourself in advance of the meeting, "Have I thought of everything?"
2. "Have I kept a progress checklist and kept it up to date?" If not, bring it up to date *before* the meeting gets underway. Most of us like to think we have good memories and a fine eye for detail, and most of us do, but it is beyond the realm of human retentive powers to have all the details involved in running a successful meeting filed neatly in your head. That's why checklists, which probably will be pretty ratty looking before the opening gun, are all-important. They jog the memory, as

well as serve as launch pads for something you may have left out. Figure 1, on page 221, is a handy checklist you might want to use and update right from the first day you start planning the meeting.

3. Write everything down, and we do mean *everything* that has to do with the logistics of the meeting. How you keep track of all these notes to yourself is not important, just as long as you do keep track. If you have an efficient secretary, ask him or her to set up a sales meeting folder and to type your thoughts in readable form for the folder. This will serve a couple of purposes: a) another person will be privy to your planning and the details of it should you become ill and b) you can constantly update yourself on whether something has been taken care of by referring to the folder. It need not be an elaborately cross-indexed file, but by the day of the sales meeting it should be bulging. Make sure you review this file, note by note, the night before the meeting at the latest. We guarantee that you're going to find something that needs taking care of.

4. Check, recheck, and *recheck*. This means everything, right down to and including the outlets along the baseboards of the meeting room. Take the checklists you have been maintaining during the planning process and circle each item that has been accomplished in a red or blue pencil. That will signal that the detail has been taken care of. Take action immediately on the things which have not been circled (there will be more of these than you might imagine). Even if you have plenty of help in planning and organizing the meeting, it is important that you, as meeting manager, do this final rechecking. This is not a chore to be delegated because it is you who will take the heat if anything goes seriously wrong.

Advance planning

One of the safest ways to ensure against unpleasant last-minute foul-ups is to make sure you have arranged for buffers in all key

©Dartnell Corporation

Figure 1. Anti-emergency Checklist

Site Selection
- Name_____
- Address_____
- Phone_____
- Contact_____
- Phone_____
- Number expected_____
- Climate_____
- Accessibility_____
- _____
- _____
- Attractions_____
- _____

Housing, Reservations
- # Sleeping rooms_____
- Singles_____@$_____
- Doubles_____@$_____
- Suites_____@$_____
- Hospitality suite $_____
- Reservation forms
  - Mailed by_____
  - Confirmed on_____

Transportation
- Tickets mailed_____
- Total cost_____
- Special fares
  - Group_____
  - Special routes_____
  - Seasonal_____
  - Super savers_____
- Promotion help
  - Advertising_____
  - VIP room_____
  - Giveaways_____
  - Baggage help_____
- Airport directions_____
- Ground transport_____

To Be Shipped
- New products_____
- Film_____
- Lights_____
- Extras_____
- Who receives_____
- _____
- _____
- Method of shipping_____
- _____
- _____
- Shipping deadline_____

Meeting Room
- Number of chairs_____
- Head table_____
- Room set-up_____
- Tables_____
- Lecterns_____
- Platforms_____
- Blackboards_____
- Corkboards_____
- Easels_____
- A/V_____
- Projector table_____
- Supplier_____
- _____
- Address_____
- Phone_____

Support Services
- Lighting_____
- Outlets_____
- Spotlights_____
- Microphones_____
- PA system_____
- Phone messages_____
- Projection operator_____
- _____
- Note pads_____
- Pencils_____
- Banners_____

Food, Beverages
- Number of meals_____
- Menus_____
- Room #s_____
- Open bar?_____
- Total cost_____
- Contact_____
- _____
- Phone_____
- Head table_____
- Local laws on alcohol
- _____
- Decorations_____
- Admission procedure
- _____
- _____
- Guarantee deadline
- _____
- Photographer_____
- Entertainment_____
- _____
- _____
- Showtime_____

Speakers
- Screened_____
- Fee_____
- Name_____
- Address_____
- Phone_____
- Speaker room_____
- Intro speaker_____

Promotion
- Media advised_____
- _____
- On-site releases_____
- Pressroom_____
- Photo possibilities
- _____
- _____

©Dartnell Corporation

areas of the meeting. In military terms, always have a fall-back position. Doing this, too, requires some advance planning.

Some suggestions for protecting yourself adequately with buffers are presented here.

Extra rooms Always make sure you have extra rooms available at the meeting location. This sounds expensive, and it does cost, but if your meeting is large enough and if you are a steady customer of the hotel, you surely can work out some arrangement with the hotel management to hold several rooms past the normal cut-off time.

Most people move around at a far faster pace than they once did, particularly in the business community, and putting a precise number on the attendance may prove more difficult than it once was. A good rule of thumb to follow in the event of an overbooking problem at your meeting is to have an arrangement with the hotel to hold at least five rooms for every 100 reserved. These rooms can be released later in the evening, should your overbooking fears fail to materialize. If you are careful to release the rooms, and they become occupied by other visitors, the hotel will probably charge only a nominal amount—a percentage of the normal fee. This is another reason why it's a good idea to develop friendly, cooperative contacts with hotel personnel.

Arrange for a back-up speaker One of the most alarming emergencies that can (and does) arise at a sales meeting is the last-minute cancellation of the main speaker or trainers you had planned on. You'll save yourself a lot of grief by keeping a back-up speaker at the ready. You eventually will recover half of the fee, but not for some period of time after the meeting.

There are various methods of securing back-up speakers, and it's good to keep them in mind should weather, illness, or even death preclude the arrival of your scheduled speaker.

One of the most satisfactory means of securing a back-up speaker is to contact the local Chamber of Commerce, which maintains a speaker's bureau in most large cities. True, you may not get someone as skilled in the field as your original speaker, but you will be able to fill a major hole in your program without too much sweat. If the city

©Dartnell Corporation

is a large one, it will have experts in virtually any field ready and willing to earn a speaker's fee. The city's convention bureau, too, will doubtless maintain a directory of available speakers on almost any topic.

It is a good idea to acquaint yourself with the colleges and universities in the city wherever your meeting is to be held. All colleges and universities worth the name maintain a speaker's bureau for their academic staff, who generally are delighted to moonlight at sales meetings. Frequently the speakers available at colleges and universities are highly professional in their field of knowledge. Note in particular that, with the recent advent of more scientific management procedures, economics professors have come a long way from only parochial knowledge of how our systems work. Most of these speakers, too, will be quite willing to adapt their talk to your specific needs, if you give them at least a little notice.

Don't put a back-up speaker on stage cold turkey. Too risky. Make sure you spend a little time with the person to make your goals clear. He or she will appreciate this courtesy and tailor the remarks to your audience.

In the eventuality of the speaker getting snowed in or ill, the problem usually can be solved with dispatch. But don't wait until the last minute to determine if the city has a major university or if the Chamber of Commerce has a speaker's bureau. Determine that long in advance of the actual meeting.

Plan for meal flexibility

Almost anything can go wrong in the kitchens of major hotels, and frequently it does. Turnover is great in most hotel food service operations, and you must keep this in mind in meal planning. Try to keep the menus and method of service as simple as possible. A skeleton staff of waiters can handle simple service better than a menu calling for too much individual attention.

Be prepared to be flexible, too, if you suddenly find that you have underbooked for a meal, particularly a banquet setting. Accept the fact that some of the diners will have to dine from a different menu, or choose from the entrees available from the hotel's dining room menu. Remember that supplying the numbers accurately to the banquet manager is your responsibility. And if the menu requires special touches (costly), the kitchen will have little or nothing to spare for extra place settings.

The best way to handle this, should it happen, is to admit frankly that you got the numbers wrong, or that you hadn't planned on late arrivals. The alternative to flexibility in this situation is to order more than the estimated number. This will cost the full-rate per head at most hotels and can result, also, in preparation and serving delays.

Equipment back-ups

Always have back-ups ready in case of equipment failure. This is probably the most frequent emergency encountered at a sales gathering, and it can be a major brouhaha—unless you are prepared.

The best way to be prepared, short of having doubles for everything (cost prohibitive) is to know and trust your local supplier. Shopping for the cheapest in this field is penny-wise and pound-foolish. Your hotel contact will be a good source for a reliable equipment supplier, and it's a good idea to take this person's advice. If the supplier gets business from hotel recommendations, the firm is not likely to traffic in faulty equipment.

When you have your first meeting with the supplier, don't hesitate to bring up the flip side of the deal. Ask what happens if this thing doesn't work when you need to go on. Don't accept bland reassurances on this matter. Find out if the supplier has back-up equipment nearby and someone to get it to you in a hurry. Include such a guarantee in your written agreement with the supplier.

If the hotel supplies the equipment as part of the meeting package, make sure you ask the same question about back-ups. Spell this out in the agreement before signing it. These days many meetings rely heavily on complex electronic equipment of one kind or another. The more complex, as a rule, the more likely something will go wrong.

The long pauses we've all sat through at meetings due to equipment failure or malfunction leave a sour taste in everyone's mouth and can put a chill on what began as an upbeat session.

Remember Murphy's Law: Anything that has moving parts will break down. Back-ups are essential.

Always have extras of everything

When you are packing at your office to leave for the sales meeting, forward an extra carton of those nitty-gritty things you know the hotel will supply (pencils, paper), just in case. The carton needn't be huge and should contain only basics. It is true that you will be able to secure such items locally, but at what cost in time?

If you are taking your own projector, don't court fate by going with only one bulb. As for extension cords, sometimes hotels make a federal case about coming up with one. Have a few of your own in that last-minute case you pack. In sum, double up on the most obvious things; they're the ones you will miss the most when not at hand.

Take a first-aid kit

You're not a doctor or a nurse, of course, but a first-aid kit close at hand can be mighty comforting when needed. The odds are that, with a large group of people in one room for several days, you'll need the kit at least once during the sessions. Once the group knows you have one, you may find yourself with some customers both before and after the formal sessions of the meeting. Few people think to travel with first-aid kits, yet many people are prone to minor accidents.

Section 23

Handling Problem Individuals

No meeting, unfortunately, would be complete without some confrontations with problem individuals. Face it; these people are just a percentage of the population, a percentage that is constant—whether in sales or in supermarket lines. The best advice on this sort of individual is, *be prepared*. Don't kid yourself and think your group is one big jolly family. Remember the percentage figure, a constant in the population whatever the profession, background, or demographic group.

There are all kinds of problem individuals, of course, ranging from the psychotic to those just mildly eccentric. Usually, you'll encounter only members of the latter group at any sales meeting and, within limits of good manners, there's nothing wrong with a little mild eccentricity. In fact, some of your best people may be, in your view, a little off the wall. It is true that talent in sales, as in other fields, sometimes goes in tandem with a little different way of looking at things. Often the mildly eccentric, if guided, can offer a lot to most gatherings, because they can't be programmed to look at any situation in a routine way.

However, being eccentric can be more than just following a different drummer. At a sales meeting, if carried to extremes, it can be annoying and even disruptive.

Difficult people

The most frequently encountered difficult people at sales meetings usually fall into these categories.

1. *The heckler.* This is the guy or gal who likes to argue about every point you make and sometimes in a disparaging

manner. He or she has something to say on any topic, and it usually is negative. The best way to handle this person is to keep your cool. He or she gets kicks from seeing anger, so never react in this fashion to the heckler. Very likely this type will anger the other salespeople in the room, as well as you, by constant, negative interruptions. Instead of responding to each digression, turn the comment over to the group for analysis and comment. A judgment from peers usually cools this type. If it doesn't, take this person aside and try to see what's bothering him or her. Then ask for cooperation. Some hecklers are not aware of how disruptive they are.

2. *The silent ones.* These come in at least a couple of varieties: the shy and the bored. If the person obviously is shy, compliment him or her when the person does respond. Call on the person by name and ask for an opinion. In other words, give the person's self-confidence a boost if possible.

The bored individual usually needs to be drawn out, which is no easy task. Ask for this person's opinion on something on which he or she claims to be an expert. However, care should be exercised here. The rest of the group may resent the special attention being shown to someone who is not cooperative. Sometimes it is best with a person who appears obviously bored just to let that person enjoy the boredom. A talk in private later will then be in order.

3. *The resentful one.* This may be the most common type of difficult individual these days. Usually this person comes from the ranks of the older salespeople and his or her resentments spring from a feeling of insecurity, a feeling that perhaps he or she is not keeping up with the times or the firm's technology. Attempt to draw this person out of these fears by calling on his or her experiences, many of which will be valuable to some of the younger members of the staff. Ask for this person's opinion frequently and tell anecdotes about some of his or her sales adventures. It's also

a good idea to talk over sales ideas with such a person outside the meeting. Generally, the resentful person actually is on your side, but is fearful that he or she is not included anymore.

4. *The griper.* This person, well known to all sales managers, usually is harboring some grudge or fancied slight that you may know nothing about. The first problem is to find out what the problem is, and then correct it if it's within your power to do so. Usually the griper is not angry with you or anyone in the room, but with some real or fancied slight of the past that was not addressed at the time. Find out in private what this was, and then correct it if you can. Don't dismiss the gripe as trivial. Instead, put off the solution for the sake of the meeting's progress and promise you will look into it.

5. *The talkative one.* This is the person who has fallen in love with the sound of his or her own voice. Of all difficult people at a sales meeting, this person can be the most annoying. Above all, don't embarrass this person with a squelch. Assign a job to keep the talker busy, fail to recognize him or her, or ask a tough question. Interrupt the talker who gets off onto a speech. If none of these tactics work, the other salespeople in the room likely will take care of matters by shutting up the person.

6. *The conversationalist.* This person whispers or talks to others while you conduct the meeting. He or she may be discussing what you are talking about but probably is not. Call on the person for comment on what you have just said. You likely will have to repeat yourself, but it will draw this individual's attention to the fact that he or she is being rude. If all else fails, speak to the conversationalist outside the room and ask for cooperation. He or she may not even be aware how distracting his or her behavior is.

7. *The helper.* This is the person who sincerely thinks he or she is helping you out, when actually the distraction is just

keeping others from participating. Treat this person as you would the excessive talker by questioning others and giving others assignments. Use this person later for summarizing. Don't use sarcasm in controlling this person. By doing so you can easily turn him or her into the resentful type, and that's a more serious problem to you than the person trying to help.

8. *The stubborn one.* This is the person who's convinced he or she is right 100 percent of the time—a difficult type, indeed. The best way to slow this person down is to ask the group to comment on his or her ideas. In this way, the stubborn one may come to realize that there can be several roads to Rome. If the person persists and thus slows down the meeting, move on and promise to discuss the matter in private later.

9. *The apple polisher.* Fortunately, this type has gone out of vogue in recent years, but once in a while you'll encounter one and be embarrassed by his or her effusive endorsement of anything and everything you say. By no means succumb to this person's flattery, or you stand the chance of losing the group. Watch out, too, that he or she doesn't give you a false sense of security. Pass this person over as much as possible in an attempt to get more objective opinions and comments.

10. *The rambler.* Very few of us think fast on our feet, but some are worse at rambling on and on than others. This person invariably means well and might even have some good ideas, but they are lost in a snowstorm of digressions. The best way to handle this person is to suggest that *we* are getting off the subject and need to get back before time runs out. A couple of times of doing this should do the trick.

Put them on the program

One of the best ways I've found to handle individuals who may be disruptive is to put them on the program. Here's an example. One of my more senior reps (I'll call him George) was violently opposed to any price increases on any of our products. George would tell everyone at the sales meeting that a higher price would upset the wholesaler and retailer, and, of course, the consumer would just stop buying the product if the retail price exceeded its current 49 cents! This was at a time of inflation, when all prices were rising. I dreaded the next sales meeting, because our company was raising prices again. What would I do about George?

Here's what I did. When I received word of the price increase, I called George immediately and told him the situation. I said, "George, we're going to have a serious problem with our four new reps, because they don't know how to talk to their customers about a price increase. I want you to come to our sales meeting next week and give a ten-minute talk on how to handle the price situation. Also, George, I would like you to make several calls with each of these reps the following week, and show them how to present the information to their customers."

You can probably guess what happened. George was pleased and flattered and did a bang-up job of handling the assignment. Not a single complaint was heard from George. My "bad boy" theory says that if you keep a boy (or girl) busy enough doing something he or she enjoys, there'll be no time for mischief. Try it at your next sales meeting.

Have an answer or solution ready

Being prepared is half the battle. While you can't prepare for every problem individual, you can at least identify, before the meeting, those individuals who have a record of disruptive behavior. Take a few minutes to think about these people before the meeting starts. Ask yourself:

1. Who are they?
2. What are they likely to say or do?
3. Exactly what happened with them at the last meeting?
4. How did I handle the situation and how did it work?
5. How can I best handle what they are likely to say or do?
6. What will happen if I leave them alone?

The last question is an important one, because you're sometimes better off doing nothing. This is especially true when others in the room tend to ignore the disruptive person. On the other hand, you must be sensitive to everyone else in the room, because they may expect you to do something to correct the situation.

Enlist the aid of others

Every sales group has its peer leaders. This is sometimes an older person or a top performer. Sometimes you can ask one or more of these peer leaders to help you with a problem individual. This can be particularly effective when the peer leader is respected or admired by the trouble-making individual. Many times all that is needed is for a peer to say, "Fred, don't interrupt the sales manager all the time, or we'll be here until midnight!"

Be very careful and discreet when using this technique. You don't want to be accused of having someone else do your dirty work. You also don't want the peer leader to feel pressured, not knowing which side to be on.

One of the keys to success in this endeavor is never to embarrass anyone. Scolding or putting down a person in front of others will not only be upsetting to the individual but will also make others uncomfortable. Do your criticizing in private and never punish the entire group for the misdeeds of a few. Remember always that you're running a business, not an army.

Take a look at yourself

It would be interesting to know how a problem individual at your sales meetings acts at an entirely different meeting. This may be difficult to determine, but it could say something about how you run a meeting.

The biggest single reason individuals behave badly at a meeting is that they feel that they're not a part of the meeting, they're not involved, and they have no voice in what is being said or decided. Open up your meetings. Make them informal and participative, and you may be pleasantly surprised at the attitudes of those in the room.

In these times, participation and involvement are almost mandatory at any get-together. You simply must accept the reality of today. Most people, and particularly salespeople, insist that they be brought into the planning and decision-making process. They want to be heard, and they want feedback on what you think about their ideas and recommendations. In short, they want action and straight talk. That can be a refreshing change!

Section 24

Closing the Meeting

An otherwise lively, productive sales meeting can be sullied by a wind-down closing. Everyone knows that it is about to end—but when? The last two hours or so of any sales gathering can be a killer, if you don't make a point of going out with a bang, not a whimper.

Closings are always difficult to handle well, mainly because everyone has on his or her mind something else—catching the plane home, checking out, packing. The final two hours are lost, unless you plan ahead.

First, don't start the wind-down far in advance of the actual closing by using such expressions as, "Well, we're near the end." Keep going with substantive material requiring group participation right up until the final minutes.

When you close, do so fast and decisively by summarizing what took place at the gathering. This summary should run no more than five minutes. Repeat the meeting objectives and tell how they have been met. If agreements were reached, review them. Ask for final comments or questions.

If it is apparent by your actions that the questions should not be of the confrontational variety (too late for that), it is likely you will get mostly so-called housekeeping questions toward the end, such as, "What's that new telephone number again for the delivery expediter?"

End on a high note In closing, it is important to always end on a high note. Say something encouraging, positive, and cheerful. Show confidence in the future. You may wish to call upon a couple of people for comments on the meeting. This is best if pre-arranged.

©Dartnell Corporation

If you have something of outstanding group interest to announce (such as a pay raise or a better car allowance), save it for your parting shot. This provides for a particularly effective closing.

It is also a good idea to review briefly a new product's advantages for increasing sales or to highlight again the main pitch of the meeting.

Stress what is expected of everyone and be sure everyone understands. If it doesn't appear to you that everyone is clear on what is expected, ask one or more people in the room to summarize the goals and plans of the company.

Leave no doubt in anyone's mind that you will carry out the commitments you have made at the meeting and that you expect all the salespeople to do the same.

Leave a strong impression

Leaving a strong final impression in closing is imperative. One of the best means of accomplishing this is to review the firm's financial strength, its tradition of service in the industry, and its reputation of standing behind its employees and customers. If sincere—and true—this pep talk will linger in the minds of the sales personnel long after they have returned to their territories. Do not make this final impression maudlin or mere rah-rah stuff. State the facts simply and sincerely and in your own style.

You also can use the so-called surprise ending to good effect—that is, if you have a genuine surprise. For example, a couple of the people may have been promoted to regional or national jobs within the company, or one of the longtime employees who has been helpful and close to the sales force may be retiring. Call this person on stage and present him or her with a retirement gift and thanks from everyone. Make sure that your surprise is positive and one that will leave a warm, collegial feeling with everyone as they file out the door to go home.

Keep in mind that all firms are judged by their own employees on how the least among us is treated. If they've done a good job, ask the waiters to take a bow; or call on the head of housekeeping and thank her or him for all the help.

©Dartnell Corporation

Writing yourself a letter

Another good idea involves what is known as *writing a letter to yourself.* Just before the sales meeting ends and after all have agreed to the firm's goals for the future, hand out to each person a blank envelope and a sheet of paper headed Memo to Myself. Then ask each person to write down the specific things they plan to do in the next 30 days (or similar period) to carry out their commitments or to accomplish the agreed-upon goals. Next, ask each person to fold the memo and place it in the envelope, seal the envelope, and write his or her name and address on it. Collect the envelopes from everyone. Mail all of them 30 days later. This not only serves as a reminder to everyone of what took place at the sales meeting, but is a positive way to get your programs implemented.

In closing on closings, the most important things to remember are, keep it brief, keep it upbeat, and keep it punchy.

©Dartnell Corporation

Section 25

Evaluating the Meeting

There is a regrettable tendency in the sales meeting process to fold one's tent after the final gavel falls and go on about something else, while making the assumption that the recent meeting is history. This is unfortunate, because no sales meeting should be out of mind until the results have been evaluated.

In effect, you should determine how effective the meeting was as a matter of procedure. It may well be that no one is going to ask for or demand an evaluation from you; but as part of the management team, it is up to you to at least satisfy yourself that something was accomplished by the meeting.

There are two ways to look at the effectiveness of a sales meeting. The first is to evaluate the meeting on the basis of whether or not you accomplished everything you set out to do. That shouldn't be a major task if your goals and plans were specific.

The second measurement is both more difficult and more important. Did anything happen as a result of the meeting? If, for example, the meeting was for the purpose of planning a new product introduction, was the new product introduced with all the gusto and enthusiasm you could muster? While there are many other factors that contribute to the success of a new product, certainly how it is *first presented* to the sales force is critical to its successful introduction.

Actually, there should be two evaluations of any meeting. One should take place right after the meeting, the other after your salespeople have had a chance to put into practice the ideas put forth at the meeting.

©Dartnell Corporation

Did you accomplish what you had planned?

As discussed previously, it is advisable to set one primary goal for any sales meeting. Right after the meeting, you should be able to determine if this primary goal was met. It should be no problem to figure out right away if you got through the agenda you planned for the meeting. These are the two basic forms of evaluation to use during and at the end of the meeting.

It also is a good idea to distribute a form at the end of the meeting, or just as the meeting is drawing to a close, in which you ask each salesperson to make his or her own evaluation. This works well in large groups, particularly in cases where the boss can't be expected to recognize each individual's handwriting.

Suggested forms for evaluation by the salespeople appear in Figures 1 and 2 on pages 239 and 240. (Also refer to a slightly different evaluation form shown in Section 3.)

Has sales performance improved?

Evaluating the results of the sales meeting after the salespeople have returned to their territories and have had a chance to put into practice what they may have learned at the meeting is not an easy thing to do, unless your firm has the capability of monitoring sales by item on a daily basis and unless your salespeople have close supervision either from you or divisional managers.

A perfectly admirable product, priced right, well promoted, and packaged attractively, very well might languish in the press of following up on reorders, unless you spot this trend early. The best and easiest method to stop such a trend, of course, is to have a daily post-meeting handle on sales figures. Is the new item being placed widely? You can find this out from sales reports, of course, but the far better way to monitor this is to watch the reorder demand. A new item introduced at the meeting might take off like a bolt in initial orders, then languish on the shelves.

Regarding the salespeople's utilization of the sales techniques recommended at the meeting, try to work closely with as many of the salespeople as possible. Are they putting some of the theory expounded at the meeting into practice, or are they resisting changes from their former habits? The answer to this question has a lot to do

©Dartnell Corporation

Figure 1. Meeting Evaluation Form

(Use scale of 1 to 10, 10 being tops)

Preparation

1 2 3 4 5 6 7 8 9 10

Reasons_____

_____

Meeting flow

1 2 3 4 5 6 7 8 9 10

Reasons_____

_____

Satisfaction with decisions made

1 2 3 4 5 6 7 8 9 10

Reasons_____

_____

Accommodations

1 2 3 4 5 6 7 8 9 10

Reasons_____

_____

Suggestions for improvement_____

_____

_____

_____

Other comments_____

_____

_____

No Signature Necessary

©Dartnell Corporation

Figure 2.

> WE NEED YOUR HELP! In order that we may make future training sessions better, we want and need your ideas, suggestions, and constructive criticism. Please be completely frank and honest in your opinions.
>
> 1. Name of training session_____
>   Date_____ Position_____
>   How long with company?_____
> 2. What subjects presented during the training session could be eliminated or the time devoted to them reduced?
> 3. Which parts of the program were of most help to you?
> 4. What subjects presented during the training session should be expanded?
> 5. What areas of discussion or subjects should be added to the program?
> 6. How would you rank the value of the program to you?
>   Excellent_____ Good_____ Fair_____ Waste of time_____
> 7. In your opinion, was the scheduling of your attendance timely? Should it have been earlier or later in your career? Why?_____
>   _____
> 8. Please give us any miscellaneous comments or suggestions which you feel may be of help._____
>   _____
>
> NOTE: It is not necessary that this questionnaire be signed.
>
> THANK YOU!!

with how successful (effective) the sales meeting was in getting through to the sales force.

Figure 3, on page 241, shows a handy form the sales supervisor can use, when working with salespeople, to determine how much of what they learned is being used.

However you evaluate, go into the process with a real desire to get to the truth. Avoid the temptation to prove yourself right, even if the evidence is overwhelming that you are not. Evaluate with an inquiring mind, not in the mood of proving anyone right or wrong. The reason for evaluation, and it's a good one, is to point the way to how you can do better next time.

When all is said and done, most sales managers know whether

Figure 3. In-Field Review of Sales Meeting Goals and Plans

> Instructions: The sales supervisor will complete this form at the conclusion of the work-with, discussing it with the salesperson at that time. One copy is to be forwarded to the sales manager.
>
> Name of salesperson_____ Date of this work-with_____
>
> Prepared by sales supervisor_____ Date of sales meeting_____
>
> What action(s) was this salesperson to take as a result of the above-listed sales meeting?
>
> _____
>
> What is this salesperson's *understanding* of what he or she is to do as a result of the above-listed sales meeting?
>
> _____
>
> What did the sales supervisor observe the salesperson doing or accomplishing in relation to the action(s) outlined at the sales meeting?
>
> _____
>
> Other comments by sales supervisor   Comments of salesperson
>
> _____
>
> What goals or plans have been agreed to as a result of this work-with?
>
> _____
>
> Signed: Sales supervisor_____
>
> Salesperson_____

the meeting was successful. It's an instinct possessed by those who run the meeting. This self-evaluation, if honest, probably is the most pertinent to the evaluation process.

What to evaluate

Here are some guidelines on what to evaluate at a sales meeting:
- Was there adequate preparation?
- Was there good participation?
- Were the presentations professionally done?
- Were the accommodations okay, superior, or not so hot?
- Were the primary objectives reached?
- Were the speakers effective?
- Did you stick to the schedule?
- Did you stay within budget?
- Was the general tone upbeat?
- Have there been measurable results?

©Dartnell Corporation

Rather than have your salespeople check off boxes and give 1 to 10 ratings, you may want to use a sentence completion form. I first learned of this excellent evaluation technique from Rodger Davenport, Director of Sales Personnel for American Greetings Corporation. Figures 4 and 5, pages 243 and 244, show examples of how this technique may be used to evaluate field management and industrial sales managers.

It takes a bit longer to complete, but the answers are more useful than those from a "happiness rating." For example, one of Rodger's sentences to be completed is, "When my boss asks me about this sales meeting, I'll say—" (leave several lines for completion). It's best to mix the sentence completion items with regular questions, like, "Which part of the meeting was most interesting to you?"

Figure 4. Field Management Seminar

Complete the following sentences:

1. Probably the greatest single benefit I derived from this school was _____

2. The subject was _____

3. Management theories are OK, but my job requires a really practical approach. In this week, I will _____

4. When my boss asks me about this week, I think I'll say _____

5. The biggest change I'll make back home _____

6. I was disappointed we didn't have more time for _____

7. There were some subjects where the time was not properly utilized, such as _____

8. I would really like to know more about _____

9. Two days on financial matters were _____

10. The subject that made the biggest impression was _____

11. The after-hours discussion with other participants could have been _____

12. The one thing that really bothers me is _____

13. If I were in charge of planning future field management seminars, I would _____

14. My feeling about the overall program as it applies to my job assignment and future goals is _____

©Dartnell Corporation

Figure 5. Industrial Sales Seminar

Complete the following sentences:

1. Probably the greatest single benefit I derived from this seminar was_____

2. Theories are OK, but my job requires a really practical approach and this seminar_____

3. When my boss asks me about this seminar, I think I'll say_____

4. In terms of value to me, my initial reaction is_____

5. As a follow-up to this seminar, it's my opinion that_____

6. I was disappointed that you didn't have more time for_____

7. I would really like to know more about_____

8. When I talked to the others at this session, we concluded that_____

9. The subject that made the biggest impression was_____

10. If I were planning an industrial sales seminar, I would_____

11. It seems to me you could have_____

12. My feeling about this past week as it applies to my present job and future goals is_____

©Dartnell Corporation

Index

Agenda, 9, 21-24
    request form, 22
    sales meeting, form, 25
American Hotel & Motel Association, 124
American Management Association, 130
American Society for Training Development, 130
Announcing the meeting, 49-53
Audio-visual aids, 17

Budget, meeting, 11-17
    forms, 13-14
    preparing, 12
Buzz sessions, 43

Closing the meeting, 233-235
Consultants as meeting planners, 123
Contest winners meetings, 76
Costs
    banquet/food, 210
    sales meeting, 11-17
    speaker fees, 135-136
Customer knowledge, 86

Dial Corporation, 87
Difficult people, dealing with, 227-232

Emergency meeting planning, 219-225
    anti-emergency checklist, 221
    and speaker cancellation, 222
    suggestions for, 219-225
Entertainment planning, 157, 215-218
Exhibit Designers & Producers Association, 124

Fear of speaking, 167
Films as training tool, 65

©Dartnell Corporation

Food/banquet functions, 16, 205-214, 223
    alcohol service, 211, 213
    banquet tips, 207-208
    cost negotiations, 210
    food function planner form, 206
    luncheon buffet, 207
    meal guarantees/forms, 210-212
    menu checklist form, 214
    menu planning, 209

Group discussions, 69

Higgins, Ray, 87
Hotel Sales & Marketing Association
    International, 124
Hotels, 16, 149-158
    accommodations/meeting room checklist, 153
    catering functions checklist, 155
    contracts, 154
    equipment supplied by, 156
    letters to, 150
    and meeting size, 153
    negotiating with, 149-158
Humor, 95-108
    ethnic & racial taboos, 96
    jokes & one-line ad libs, 98-108
    rules for using, 96-98

Ice breakers for meetings, 160
Infomart, 124
International Association of Conference Centers,
    144-147
Introductions, meeting, 161

Jokes for meetings, 98-108

Lecture skills, 56-58

Media specialist, 123
Meeting evaluation forms, 25, 239-241, 243-244
Meeting objective checklist, 46
Meeting planners, 119-124
    company employee as, 122
    consultants, 122, 124
    inside, 122
    outside, 121
    media specialist, 123
Meeting planning, 19-29
    goals, 20
    objectives, 19
Meeting rooms, 195-204
    auditorium/theater style, 196-197
    conference table, 196-199
    emergencies, 195
    equipment, 203-204, 224
    furniture, 196-200
    lighting, 200
    physical layout, 196
    schoolroom style, 200-201
    ventilation, 202
Meeting site, 137-147
    airport, 141, 143-144
    checklist, 27, 142
    conference centers, 144-147
    convention bureau aid in choosing, 138
    questions to ask, 137, 140
    selection, 26-28, 141
Motivation, 8

National Society of Sales Training Executives, 130
New product introduction, 8, 75, 84

Participation, meeting, 39-47
    planning, 41
    self-evaluation checklist, 47
    techniques, 43-44
Pre-meeting assignments for salespeople, 163

Presentation, meeting, 165-186
    goal of, 165
    planning, 169-172
    types of, 165-167
    worksheets, 185-186
Problem solving, 8, 43
Publicity for sales meetings, 51-53

Role Playing, 44, 65-67

Sales & Marketing Executives International, 124
Sales meetings
    agenda, 9, 21-24
    closing, 233, 235
    difficult people, dealing with, 227-232
    emergency planning, 219-225
    entertainment planning, 215-218
    evaluation of, 45-47, 237-244
    food & banquet considerations, 205-214
    humor in, 95-108
    objectives of, 9, 19
    opening techniques for, 159-164
    participation in, 39-47
    planning, 19-29
    presentations, 165-186
    purpose of, 7-10
    rooms, 195-204
    themes, 31-38
    types of, 71-78
Sales training quiz, 68
Self-evaluation checklist, 47
Showmanship in meetings, 109-117
Society of Corporate Professionals, 124
Speakers, 132-136, 167-169
    choosing, 133
    college bureaus as source for, 16
    and delivery, 173
    emergency cancellation of, 222
    fees, 135-136
    introducing the, 183
    meeting outline for, 127
    outside, 134

©Dartnell Corporation

Speakers (continued)
    and questions from audience, 184
    sources for recruiting, 133
    tips, 172
    using pauses, 174
    and voice control, 176

Speaking skills, 180-181
Speaking tips, 167-169, 172-173
Speeches, content of, 177-179
Stunts and gimmicks for meetings, 162

Telephone conference calls, 75, 77
Television as training tool, 60-65
Themes for meetings, 31-38
    advantages of, 31
    ideas for, 38
    selecting, 32
    theme building concepts, 33-37

Topic suggestions for meetings form, 42
Trainers, choosing, 129
Training needs of sales force, 128
Training program, 131
Training techniques and meetings, 55-70
Training needs/priorities form, 126
Travel arrangements, 15, 187-193
    airline reservation form, 189
    ground transportation, 192
    group travel, 190
    hotels, 16
    hub cities, 187
    payment for, 188

Visual aids, 181-182

Workshop leaders, 17, 125-132
Workshop/seminars, 43, 58, 79-93
    action form, 59
    ideas, 83
    presentation building, 85
    topics, 82, 93
    work plan, 89-90

©Dartnell Corporation

Sharpen Your Management Skills with These Practical Guides from Dartnell

1. Copywriting Secrets & Tactics
Herschell Gordon Lewis, 255 pp. Text; 150 pp. Advertising Workshop; 3-Ring Binder; 50 illustrations; $91.50
Cut through the advertising and sales clutter with hundreds of examples and tricks of the trade to make all your sales messages come alive and stand out from the crowd. Get the inside tips on how to:
- Open sales copy with a bang
- Make headlines get attention every time
- Sell with features and benefits
- Use the "little words" that mean a lot when closing the sale

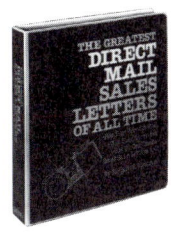

2. The Greatest Direct Mail Sales Letters of All Time
Dick Hodgson, 450 pp.; 3-Ring Binder; $91.50
No matter what your market is—business-to-business, industrial, consumer goods, service—you'll be on your way to higher responses and bigger sales with your own personal file of sure-fire sales builders. More than 100 examples of the letters that have made the greatest impact and garnered the best responses ever are included—with commentary—in this one-of-a-kind sales writers' reference.

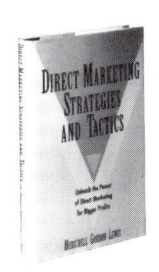

3. Direct Marketing Strategies and Tactics
Herschell Gordon Lewis, 370 pp.; Hardcover; $49.95
Put yourself on the inside track to profits in direct marketing by knowing how to use **all** the forms of direct marketing to squeeze the highest possible response from your programs. This is the complete guide to learning how to:
- Target markets and customers
- Pick the right media
- What to "learn" from tests
- Use order cards, envelopes, and follow-up phone calls to increase response.

Plus 170 "Impact Ideas" put these tips into practice today.

4. Sales Manager's Handbook — 14th Ed.
John Steinbrink, 1,272 pp.; Hardcover; $49.95
Loaded with timely case studies and practical illustrations, the classic working sales manager's single-volume reference gives you more complete coverage, greater attention to detail, and more practical solutions to the sales manager's every challenge than any other single volume on the market.

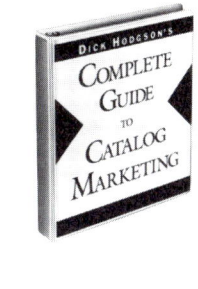

5. Complete Guide to Catalog Marketing
Dick Hodgson, 420 pp. Text; 200+ Illustrations; 32 pp. Order Form Portfolio; 16 pp. 4-color Creative Portfolio; 32 pp. Workshop; 3-Ring Binder; $91.50
Take the advice of the champion in the business before you produce your next catalog. This idea-packed manual shows you the ins and the outs of marketing successfully with catalogs. From identifying markets to choosing merchandise to creating and producing to measuring results and profitability. Loaded with hundreds of practical hints, examples, and tips in handy checklists, forms, and "swipe files."

6. Integrated Advertising
Carol Nelson, 213 pp.; Hardcover; $34.95
Combine the long-term image-building power of successful advertising with the here-and-now, profit potential of database and direct marketing in integrated advertising campaigns that work. Loaded with illustrated checklists of pitfalls to avoid, new ways to identify your audience, harnessing data-power for bigger profits. Problem-solving ideas throughout.

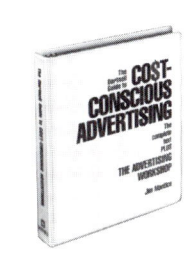

7. Cost Conscious Advertising
Jim Mantice, 320 pp. Text; 75 pp. Workshop; 3-Ring Binder; $91.50
Get better bottom-line results from all your advertising—now. Armed with the author's time-tested cost-control formula, you'll spend less and get more from your advertising expenses without sacrificing quality or response. A handy Advertising Workshop shows you how to put these cost-saving ideas into practice into your programs today.

8. T.E.A.M.S.: Together Each Achieves More Success
Jim Lundy, 230 pp.; Hardcover; $19.95
T.E.A.M.S. is a must-read for anyone seeking more profitable, productive teamwork. In 200 pages loaded with checklists, outlines for improving team effectiveness, and scores of cases and anecdotes, *T.E.A.M.S.* gives you practical approaches to making teamwork work and success-driven strategies and tactics that will make your teams work more powerfully, productively and profitably. Lundy's message shows everyone how to work together to achieve a common goal. Regardless of your company's size, Lundy's insights will get you going!

To order: fill in and mail the attached order card.

THE DARTNELL GUARANTEE
If the product you order does not meet your satisfaction, return it within 30 days for a full refund.

1 2 3 4 5 6 7 8
9 10 11 12 13 14 15 16

Circle the numbers of the titles you wish to order. (Numbers correspond to the titles shown above.)

❏ Please send me a free catalog of all Dartnell Products.

❏ Bill My Company   ❏ American Express   ❏ Master Charge   ❏ Visa

Account #   Exp. Date

Signature

Name   Title

Company Name

Address

City   State   Zip

Phone

(Signature and phone number required to process order.)

92-5508

FOR FASTER SERVICE CALL - U.S.: 1-800-621-5463
Canada: 1-800-441-7878
Fax: 312-561-3801

More Practical Management and Reference Guides from Dartnell

9. How to Create Powerful Catalog Copy
Herschell Gordon Lewis, 331 pp.; Hardcover; $49.95
One of the world's leading authorities on writing copy that sells more product lays out solid principles for making catalog copy pull—and then loads page after page with examples showing how to do it (and "not" do it). Includes handy "rules of thumb" guidelines, and checklists you can use to guarantee success at every stage of the process.

10. Questions That Make The Sale
William Bethel, 160 pp.; Paperback; $19.95
What is your most powerful selling tool? Questions! Well-timed, skillful questioning can propel you through each stage of selling to and through a successful closing. Eleven information-packed chapters show you how to rivet attention on your presentations, how to identify and clarify your customers and their needs and how to motivate, qualify, prospect, probe and close with greater success. The final chapter contains 365 questions, "a question a day" to achieve greater sales success.

11. Dartnell's 27th Sales Force Compensation Survey
250 pp.; 3-Ring Binder; Forms, Sample Plans; $199.00
Get the most performance for the money you pay your sales force. The most important step you can take toward controlling costs and improving sales productivity is here—in the longest running survey of sales compensation issues:
- Salaries, commissions, bonuses paid to 10 sales levels
- Cost and length of training
- Travel and field expenses
- Sample pay and expanse plans

More than 100 tables, tabbed for easy use, plus more than 50 sample pay plans, expense policies and job descriptions.

12. Building Sales with Demographics and Psychographics
Judith Nichols, 289 pp.; Hardcover; $29.95
Demographics. Psychographics. Buzzwords or Sales Builders? Judith Nichols shows you how to cut through the jargon and make the terms and terminology work for you—to build your business' sales and profits through better understanding of your customers' individual and group needs. You'll get the numbers and the statistics, but more important, you'll get the guidance to use them profitably.

13. Performance Driven Sales Management
George Odiorne, 260 pp. Text; 80 pp. Sales Management Workshop; 3-Ring Binder; 60 Exhibits; $91.50
Manage your sales force more profitably with this step-by-step management guide:
- Set realistic profit and performance goals
- Develop team-driven sales goals and strategies
- Measure progress fairly and accurately
- Train for maximum effectiveness

An 80-page Workshop shows these ideas in action in real-life situations.

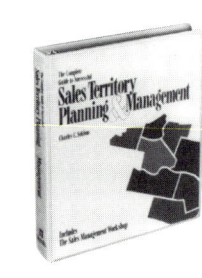

14. Complete Guide to Successful Sales Territory Planning and Management
Charles Schlom, 220 pp. Text; 130 pp. Sales Management Workshop; 3-Ring Binder; $91.50
This practical territory management guide will help you:
- Plan and manage your profitability, customers, and products
- Identify key accounts faster
- Set clearer objectives
- Measure results more accurately
- Coach your team more effectively

Workshop helps you track your growth with real-world problems and solutions.

15. Idea-A-Day Guide to Super Selling and Customer Service
Tony Alessandra, Ph.D., Gary Couture and Gregg Baron, 280 pp.; Paperback; $19.95
Sales Success in just fifteen minutes a day with the *Idea-A-Day Guide*. It's loaded with sales success ideas—250 of them—one for each working day of the year. Not just another how-to book, *Idea-A-Day's* unique organization gives you a new money-making idea on every page to give you a one-of-a-kind, hands-on reference you'll use every day of the year. Plus easy-to-use self-diagnostic test helps you measure your skills and evaluate your progress.

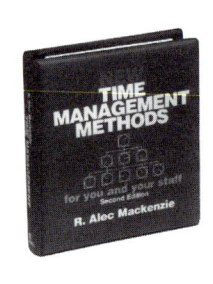

16. New Time Management Methods for You and Your Staff
R. Alex Mackenzie, 260 pp.; 3-Ring Binder; $91.50
Do more in less time. Increase the productivity of your entire team. Practical, proven time management techniques help you and your team become more efficient, effective and profitable.

BUSINESS REPLY MAIL
FIRST CLASS   PERMIT NO. 545   CHICAGO, IL
POSTAGE WILL BE PAID BY ADDRESSEE

DARTNELL
4660 N. Ravenswood Avenue
Chicago, IL 60640-9981

NO POSTAGE
NECESSARY
IF MAILED
IN THE
UNITED STATES